Strategic Weapons:

An Introduction

Strategic Weapons:

An Introduction

Norman Polmar

Revised Edition

Crane Russak • *New York*
National Strategy Information Center, Inc.

**Strategic Weapons:
An Introduction, revised edition**

Published in the United States by

Crane, Russak & Company, Inc.
3 East 44th Street
New York, NY 10017

Copyright © 1982 National Strategy Information Center, Inc.
111 East 58th Street
New York, NY 10022

Library of Congress Cataloging in Publication Data

Polmar, Norman.
Strategic weapons.

(Strategy papers; no. 38)
1. Atomic weapons.   2. Strategic forces.
I. National Strategy Information Center.
II. Title   III. Series.
UF767.P62 1981   358'.39   81-12595
ISBN 0-8448-1399-0   AACR2
ISBN 0-8448-1411-3 (pbk.)

Printed in the United States of America

Table of Contents

Preface

Many Americans are taking an increasing interest in the urgent but not easily understood issues of competition and confrontation between the United States and the Soviet Union. The interaction between the super-powers is profoundly influenced by, and to a large extent centers around, the strategic weapons possessed by both sides. Hence, a basic knowledge of these weapons is an essential key to understanding the most pressing problems of international relations today.

This volume—a revised and up-dated edition of a book by the same author first published in 1975—fills the long-standing need for a thorough but simplified layman's discussion of the whole subject of strategic weapons. The book provides a non-technical outline of the history of strategic weapons development, an inventory of presently-existing strategic weapons hardware, and a projection of possible future trends. The book concentrates on U.S. and Soviet strategic programs, but a brief chapter on the other nuclear powers is also included.

Norman Polmar is an analyst, author, and editor, specializing in U.S. and Soviet naval and strategic matters. Over the past fifteen years, he has participated in or directed major studies for various offices of the Navy, Army intelligence, the Under Secretary of Defense for research, the Defense Nuclear Agency, and the Maritime Administration, as well as for several private shipbuilding and aerospace firms. In addition, Mr. Polmar has been a prolific writer in the defense field. His most recent book is a full-length biography of Admiral H.G. Rickover, controversial head of the Navy's nuclear propulsion program. From 1967 to 1977, Mr. Polmar was editor of the United States sections of the annual *Jane's Fighting Ships*. He subsequently edited a new series of reference books for the U.S. Naval Institute Press, entitled *The Ships and Aircraft of the U.S. Fleet* and *Guide to the Soviet Navy*. Mr. Polmar also writes a regular column for the Naval Institute *Proceedings*, the professional journal of the Navy, and is a frequent contributor to other magazines and newspapers.

This book serves as an important primer for those who would enter the discussion or study of strategic weapons, and as an invaluable reference work for those already involved in this important and controversial subject. For these reasons, the National Strategy Information Center is pleased to offer this volume as a contribution to the ongoing debate concerning the larger issues of U.S.–Soviet relations.

Frank R. Barnett, *President*
National Strategy Information Center

June 1982

1

An Evolutionary Process

The stillness of the New Mexico desert was torn asunder at 5:30 a.m. on the morning of July 16, 1945, when man exploded the first atomic bomb. Less than a month later, specially modified B-29 bombers of the US Army Air Forces released the second and third nuclear weapons over Nagasaki and Hiroshima, destroying both Japanese cities. (See Figures 1-1, 1-2, and 1-3.) Another bomb was available, and still more were in production. This was the beginning of the "atomic age."

Now, more than three decades later, nuclear and thermonuclear weapons and their delivery systems have become the benchmark of national military power. Indeed, we can define a "superpower" as a nation that could be the victim of a surprise, first-strike attack by any other nation and still inflict massive retaliatory destruction on the aggressor. "Massive destruction" in this context is, as a minimum, destroying a nation's ability to function as a viable, modern society. The Department of Defense has estimated that the loss of at least 25 percent of the population and 50 percent of the industrial capacity of the Soviet Union would destroy that nation's ability to function as a modern society.

At this moment, thousands of land- and submarine-based missiles, and hundreds of bombers armed with these weapons of mass destruction, are numbered among the arsenals of the United States, the Soviet Union, Britain, France, and the People's Republic of China, while India also has demonstrated the ability to produce such weapons. The past three and a half decades have seen the US strategic position change from one of absolute monopoly in nuclear weapons—first to a posture of overwhelming superiority, and then to the situation beginning in the 1970s, when the USSR achieved "parity" or "comparability" with the United States in certain measurements of nuclear striking power, and superiority in others. As this decline took place in the strategic position of the United States vis-a-vis the Soviet Union, US strategy changed. At the end of World War II, the defeated Axis nations and many of the victorious allied countries were devastated, their economies and industrial capabilities unable to support even a peacetime society. In terms of war-fighting capability, the USSR possessed a large and well-armed ground force that could easily have overrun Western Europe, or possibly even China. The USSR was unable to sustain such a force, however, because of catastrophic conditions in the homeland, nor did it have a long-range air or naval capability to support an aggressive national strategy.

The prevalent strategic view in the Truman phase of the air "atomic age" (1945-53) was that long-range bombers carrying nuclear weapons against enemy cities or military forces could defeat any nation or force hostile to the United States and its interests. In this environment, the US Air Force was established as a separate service, and the Army and Navy were reduced essentially to "token" forces. These small ground and naval services would be required in future conflicts primarily to provide certain occupation and logistic forces to support the primary weapon: the long-range bomber.

On June 25, 1950, ground and air forces of Communist North Korea crossed the border into South Korea in an all-out assault to gain control over the entire Korean peninsula. The perceived US strategy was articulated by one Air Force Officer who, when told that US ground troops were to be committed to the war, is said to have remarked: "The old man [General MacArthur] must be off his rocker. When the Fifth Air Force gets to work on them, there will not be a North Korean left in North Korea."

Only after three full years of conventional warfare, involving mostly US air, ground, and naval weapons of World War II vintage, was the Korean War finally brought to a conclusion. US forces had achieved their goal of maintaining the independence of South Korea without the employment of "tactical" or "strategic" nuclear weapons. Both uses were considered: tactical, in the sense of direct support to ground operations (against troop concentrations, bridges, and so forth); and strategic, against mainly factories and assembly areas in North Korea and Manchuria. President Truman apparently gave consideration to the use of nuclear weapons against the Soviet Union in this period. A journal kept in his own handwriting has an entry dated January 27, 1952, contemplating a threat of an "all out war" against the Soviet Union as well as China: "It means that Moscow, St. Petersburg [Leningrad], Vladivostok, Peking, Shanghai, Port Arthur, Dairen, Odessa, Stalingrad, and every manufacturing plant in China and the Soviet Union will be eliminated."

After the Korean War ended in stalemate in mid-1953 the war in Indochina, between French forces and the Communist Vietminh, continued in a deadly struggle. A large French force was surrounded by the Vietminh at Dienbienphu, with the end of the Korean War freeing guns, munitions, and technical advisors for the fight against the French. By the spring of 1954 the situation at Dienbienphu was critical and the French asked for American air strikes, first conventional and then nuclear (under the code name Vulture). B-29s flying from the Philippines or carrier aircraft could have carried out the strikes. Although President Eisenhower, the Secretary of State, and four of the five members of the U.S. Joint Chiefs of Staff favored direct intervention, British opposition and French reluctance to accept American direction led to an end of Operation Vulture. Dienbienphu fell to the Communists on May 7, 1954. It was a severe military defeat for the French and—more importantly—led to a political end of the conflict.

At the time the same nuclear weapons would have been used against tactical targets (Korea and Indochina) and strategic targets (the Soviet Union and China). Although American scientists during this period were developing relatively small nuclear weapons, at the time of Truman's journal entry the atomic bombs available were few in number and large in size. The Mk 3 and Mk 4 weapons then in the inventory were more than ten feet long, five feet in diameter, and weighed over five tons. Under normal circumstances, the bombs were not assembled; to put them together required a crew of trained technicians and almost a day.

As the Cold War increased in intensity, President Truman ordered an increase in nuclear weapons production. The American arsenal grew from perhaps seven bombs—or, more accurately, the components for seven— in mid-1947, to about 25 a year later, and to some 50 in mid-1949. Indications are that by mid-1950 production had provided an arsenal of at least 300, with approximately another hundred being added each year during the Korean War, and even more after that—possibly even totalling as many as 2,000 by mid-1955. Under the Truman Administration there occurred not only an increase in numbers, but a diversification of types: the Mk 5, which weighed only 3,000 pounds, had retractable fins, and was the first nuclear weapon that could be carried externally on an aircraft; the Mk 6 (8,500 pounds), which was the first to be mass produced; the small, 1,600-pound Mk 7 that could be used as a missile warhead as well as a bomb; and the Mk 8 (3,300 pounds), which was intended to penetrate hardened structures. All four weapons were produced from 1951-52 onward. Thus, after an initial period of possessing virtually no useable nuclear capability, by the early 1950s the United States was becoming a true nuclear power.

Subsequently, the Eisenhower-Dulles Administration (1953-61) enunciated the strategy that became known as "massive retaliation." According to this doctrine, aggression against the United States or its allies would be deterred with the threat of massive retaliatory nuclear strikes; if deterrence should fail, the US would prevail against the Soviet Union in a general war. The doctrine, however, also called for conventional forces to deter or contain localized aggression without resorting to nuclear weapons. While the mix and balance of conventional forces and nuclear weapons were not specified in the major policy documents, the Army and Navy both sought to modernize and maintain large conventional forces. This, in turn, further reinforced proponents of nuclear weapons as a means of controlling defense spending through the use of a relatively small Air Force and Navy nuclear attack forces. In this period, the ability of the Soviet Union to attack the United States with nuclear weapons consisted of a few long-range Soviet nuclear bombers that would have to survive both the long flight to the United States (no bases in the Western hemisphere being available) and the expanding US warning and air defense system. Also, in the 1950s an active US civil defense program was in existence.

The shift in Soviet strategy to wars of national liberation and other less direct offensive actions in the 1960s led to a corresponding change in US strategy during the Kennedy-Johnson period (1961-69) to what was called "strategic deterrence." A direct Soviet attack against the United States, and possibly against the NATO countries, would be countered by a US nuclear strike; conventional military forces, on the other hand, would be

US-USSR STRATEGIC WEAPONS LIMITATIONS
1972 AGREEMENT

	United States	Soviet Union
Large ICBMs	54	313
Light ICBMs	1,000	1,305
Submarine-Launched Ballistic Missiles (SLBMs)	710	950
Strategic Missile Submarines	44	62

(The above are the maximum allowable totals in each category. If the United States were to elect to reach the submarine missile limit, it would have to give up the 54 large Titan ICBMs; while to reach their submarine missile limit, the Soviets would be required to give up approximately 209 older light missiles of the SS-7 Saddler and SS-8 Sasin types, and 27 missiles in *Hotel*-class nuclear submarines.)

developed to counter Soviet or other hostile actions at a lower level of conflict. The ten-year Vietnam War exemplified this strategy, with more than half a million US troops fighting what some historians and other analysts have described as a "holding action," and with the national leadership clearly stating that tactical nuclear weapons—available in large numbers—would not be employed.

By the beginning of the Nixon Administration (1969), it was evident that the Soviet Union had embarked on a strategic weapons build-up to attain at least equality with the nuclear arsenal of the United States. At the same time, the cost of the Vietnam War in terms of dollars, popular support, and to some extent even public interest in military matters, had slowed the development in new US offensive weapons. Then, with the 1972 signing of the first agreement of the Strategic Arms Limitation Talks (SALT I) between the United States and the Soviet Union, the US leadership accepted Soviet "parity" in strategic offensive and defensive systems. Moreover, US leadership in certain other areas, especially multiple warheads for missiles and submarine-launched missiles, appeared to be temporary in view of ongoing Soviet programs.

Less explicit than Soviet "parity" or "comparability," three other factors have become evident in the strategic arms "race": (1) Soviet strategic arms development has been both independent and responsive with regard to US actions, but has not copied US developments; (2) the Soviet Union has the capability of matching or exceeding the quantity and, on a longer-term basis, the quality of US strategic forces; and (3) with the current strategic "balance," the possible use of highly selective strategic weapons or tactical nuclear weapons probably is increasing.

With respect to Soviet strategic arms development, certain Soviet weapons appear to have been developed in response to US programs. For example, many Soviet political and military leaders have implied that the US strategic bomber programs of the late 1940s and 1950s could not be matched by Soviet efforts because of technological limitations and geography (the Soviets did not have overseas bomber bases such as were then available to the United States). Accordingly, the Soviet government responded with an emphasis on intercontinental missiles, leading to US fears of a "missile gap" in favor of the USSR during the late 1950s. At the same time, certain Soviet weapon developments, such as the Fractional Orbital Bombardment Systems (FOBS) and satellite intercept systems, appear to be independent of specific existing or planned US weapons capabilities.[1]

The development and deployment of strategic weapons by the USSR has continued at a paced rate, with new generations of weapons being developed every few years and a significant number being deployed. This rate of development and production is based on both military and economic requirements generated by the Soviet leadership. With respect to the latter, the Soviets seek to maintain full employment and work at full capacity in missile, aircraft, and ship design bureaus, and in production facilities. A product line is generally continued until its replacement is ready to enter production; "gaps" in production are to be avoided even if "obsolescent" weapons must be produced. The continued manufacture into the 1980s of the Tu-20 Bear aircraft—an aircraft marginally suited for its mission when it first appeared in the skies over Russia in the late summer of 1954—is a case in point.

Strategic weapons development in the United States, while at times more intensive than in the USSR, is much more sporadic. There is virtually no long-term weapons development plan, and the various commercial (private) firms that design and produce US strategic weapons are in economic competition with one another. Warhead development is undertaken mainly by government laboratories on a more-or-less continuous basis. The various armed services propose the development of strategic-

---

1. In response to Soviet anti-satellite efforts, the United States initiated an anti-satellite program in the late 1970s.

mission aircraft, missiles, submarines, and related systems, often on the basis of industry proposals. Since the early 1960s and the adoption of the management procedures instituted by then-Secretary of Defense Robert McNamara, these service proposals are carefully scrutinized by various Department of Defense offices, the Administration and Congressional budgetary agencies, and then the various committees of the Congress itself. These many "wickets" tend to stop or significantly delay most projects, while approving very few on the original schedule.

At times, however, the United States is able to introduce new strategic weapons in a remarkably short period of time, generally as the reaction to a foreign development. This was demonstrated especially forcefully after the 1957 orbiting of the first earth satellite by the Soviet Union and the subsequent Soviet missile developments. While touting the "missile gap" between the two nations, American political and military leaders undertook a massive strategic development program that within a few years far outstripped the Soviet strategic forces.

After the Vietnam war (1964-72), the anti-military attitudes in segments of American society, inflation, and several examples of poor management within the armed forces and the Defense Department, in combination with President Carter's quest for a more peaceful world environment through arms limitations, led to a slowdown of US strategic weapons development. The advanced B-1 manned bomber was cancelled, the Trident submarine missile program faced massive cost overruns and time delays, confusion reigned over the land-mobile ICBM program (called M-X), and no firm schedule could be developed for strategic cruise missiles, either air- or submarine-launched.

While the development and deployment of US strategic weapons faced indecision and confusion at the start of the 1980s, the Soviet strategic weapons program seems to demonstrate organization and planning—one of the few areas of Soviet society where these characteristics are evident. The deployment of several advanced, multi-warhead ICBMs by the Soviet Strategic Rocket forces in the 1970s will be followed by a new-generation of ICBMs in the 1980s. The modern submarines with their long-range, multi-warhead missiles that went to sea in the 1970s are being succeeded on the building ways at Severodivinsk by the massive Typhoon series, with an improved missile predicted for the mid-1980s. Additionally, the Soviet bomber enigma continues. The supersonic Backfire remains in production, and although this bomber is probably a theater-regional weapon, in-flight refueling features could allow intercontinental ranges. Another bomber —which may have intercontinental ranges—is expected to enter service in the mid-1980s. Thus, the Soviet buildup of conventional ground forces and naval forces in recent years has not been achieved at the cost of any slowdown in Soviet strategic force development.

2

United States Monopoly

The mass destruction resulting from the first use of nuclear weapons by the United States in 1945 convinced political and military leaders of the major nations that these weapons could have a decisive role in the postwar world. Only one bomber carrying a nuclear weapon—if it could reach its target—would inflict the same damage that previously required thousands of bomber sorties.[2] Nuclear weapoins appeared at last to validate the words of airpower advocate Giulio Douhet, written more than two decades earlier:[3]

> The complete destruction of the objective has moral and material effects, the repercussions of which may be tremendous. To give us some idea of the extent of these repercussions, we need only envision what would go on among the civilian population of congested cities once the enemy announced that he would bomb such centers relentlessly, making no distinction between military and nonmilitary objectives.

The beginning of the atomic age was dominated by the fact that only the United States had nuclear weapons and the means to deliver them.

---

2. The Nagasaki bomb was a 23-kiloton weapon having the equivalent explosive power of 23,000 tons of TNT, or the payload of 4,000 B-29 sorties flown from the Mariana islands to Tokyo. The Hiroshima-type bomb had a yield of approximately 13 kilotons.

3. General Guilio Douhet, *The Command of the Air*. Originally published in Italian in 1921. English-language edition published in 1942 by Coward-McCann, Inc. (New York).

The initial delivery method was by four-engine B-29 bombers, the only delivery platform that could carry such heavy weapons (five tons for the early bombs) to targets more than a thousand miles from friendly bases. (See Figure 2-1.) Thus, within the US armed forces, the initial responsibility for strategic warfare fell within the province of the Army Air Forces (after 1947, the US Air Force).

Although the United States had a large number of B-29s available when World War II ended, most were quickly consigned to the scrap heap or "mothballed" in the Arizona desert. By 1946, when the US Strategic Air Command was established, there were only 148 B-29s in service as bombers, with about 30 of them modified to carry nuclear weapons. There were only a few atomic bombs available, all of the so-called Mk 3 or improved Nagasaki type. The Mk 3 weighed 10,300 pounds, was 128 inches long and 60 inches in diameter, and had a yield of over 20 kilotons.

During the late 1940s, several improved bomber aircraft were introduced into the US strategic arsenal. First came the B-50, an improved version of the piston-engine B-29, and then the long-range B-36, a piston-engine giant that could, under ideal conditions, fly a round-trip of 10,000 miles with a single early nuclear weapon. Even more significant, production of the B-47, a sleek jet bomber of medium range, was initiated in 1947.

Although the actual capabilities of American strategic bombers were limited by the numbers of nuclear weapons available and the numbers of operational aircraft, the public perception of the atomic bomber force was one of awesome power. This perception was ably abetted by Air Force publicists, the impressive size and designs of the new bombers, and continued demonstrations of bomber "capabilities." In May 1947, for example, a force of 101 B-29s flew over New York City in a "maximum mission effort" to demonstrate the striking power of the US nuclear arsenal. This was one-third of current US strategic bomber strength; another 30 B-29s planned for the mission remained at their bases because of maintenance and supply problems. In a comparably impressive demonstration, a single B-50 flew around the world in March 1949 without landing, being refueled four times in flight by a KB-29 tanker aircraft. These flights, as well as overseas flights by smaller detachments of B-29s, were intended for training as well as to demonstrate the capabilities of the Strategic Air Command (SAC), which operated the US strategic bombers.

The first confrontation with the Soviet Union in which SAC was directed to prepare for a nuclear strike was the Berlin crisis of June 1948, when the Soviets interdicted Allied ground and canal transit to the city. One B-29 squadron was already in West Germany on a training flight; and a short time later, additional B-29 squadrons were flown into West German and British air bases. Some 90 B-29s were forward-based in Europe during the crisis period.

According to US Air Force histories, however, the B-29s dispatched to Europe in 1948 were not capable of carrying atomic bombs. There were in SAC at the time only 32 B-29s modified to deliver nuclear weapons. All of them were assigned to the 509th Bomb Group, which was not deployed to Britain until the summer of 1949. (Nonnuclear components of atomic bombs were not sent to Britain until 1950, and the nuclear components apparently were not stored in Britain until the mid-1950s.) Had the decision been made to strike the Soviet Union or East Germany with nuclear weapons, several hours would have been required to assemble the bombs, and several more to load and ready the aircraft at bases in the United States. The B-29s would then have had to stage through bases in Britain to be refuelled before going on to their targets. This was a ponderous process, but still the world's only nuclear strike capability.

Airlift rather than atomic bombs became the allied strategy for the "Battle of Berlin." Consideration of US nuclear strike options did, however, point up a number of limitations in SAC capabilities, among them: (1) the limited range of aircraft, (2) the inability to store nuclear weapons overseas (even in England), and (3) the lack of ready overseas bases.

Weapons and Targets

The Soviet assaults—political and military—into Eastern Europe and the Balkans, the initial Soviet reluctance to withdraw troops from northern Iran, and other actions led to initiation in the United States of mass production of atomic bombs and acceleration of bomber production. In late 1950, when the first atomic bomb components were sent out of the country (to Britain), SAC had 520 bombers: 286 B-29s, 196 B-50s, and 38 of the giant B-36s. (See Figures 2-2, 2-3, and 2-4.) Only some 85 of the B-29s were configured to carry nuclear weapons, as were the other planes, a total of just over 300 nuclear-capable aircraft. There were perhaps 400 atomic bombs available for the planes that could carry them. Thus, the strategic bombing effort in this period would still have had a large number of B-29s delivering conventional bombs against targets in the Soviet Union.

Those targets were to be cities in the USSR whose destruction would result in the loss of Soviet industry and military resources. The earliest target list—dated November 3, 1945—listed 20 cities, led by Moscow, Gorkiy, and Kuibyshev. The loss of the 20 cities would, it was estimated, result in the destruction of 90 percent of Soviet aircraft production capability, 88 percent of truck production, 86 percent of tank production, 67 percent of crude oil, 65 percent of refined oil, etc. Obviously, it would have been necessary in 1945 to destroy the target cities with conventional bombs.

By late 1950—when some 400 atomic bombs were available— the target list had grown to 70 cities whose destruction, it was estimated, would destroy a considerably larger portion of the Soviet Union's arsenal and industry. The number of bombs to be dropped varied from eight on Moscow and seven on Leningrad to only one on some of the lesser cities.

Jet Bombers

In 1951, the capability of SAC was improved when the first large B-36s became operational (ten years after contract and three years after first delivery) and the first jet-propelled B-47s were being delivered. The B-36 was big and slow (440 m.p.h. maximum), but could reach the Soviet Union from US bases without in-flight refueling. The B-47 could accelerate to 630 m.p.h. carrying a nuclear weapon, but lacked the range to reach the Soviet Union from bases in the United States. (See Figure 2-5.) Accordingly, several SAC bases were established in Britain and Morocco in 1950-51, and large numbers of KC-97 tanker aircraft were procured to provide the B-47s with in-flight refueling. (See Figure 2-6.)

The B-36 was a large airplane (almost 360,000 pounds gross for the D model) powered by six piston engines supplemented by four jet engines in wing pods. Its size and cost made it the most-publicized bomber of the immediate postwar era. Still, its development was predictable, inasmuch as the Air Force continually sought larger bombers that could lift a greater payload of bombs and fuel.

On the other hand, the sleek E-47 was, in the words of Bill Gunston, a leading aviation historian, "a design so advanced technically as to appear genuinely futuristic." The B-47 pushed the US Air Force into the jet bomber age. Designed by the Boeing Aircraft Company, which had produced the famed B-17 and B-29 bombers, the aircraft was one of several designs considered at the end of World War II for the initial generation of jet-propelled bombers. After studying a number of configurations, Boeing engineers took advantage of German research into swept-back wings to produce the final B-47 concept. The pilot and copilot sat in tandem in a narrow fuselage, with a navigator/bombardier in the nose— a total of three men compared to ten for the B-17 and 11 for the B-29, both smaller aircraft. Space and weight instead were allocated to fuel, with the B-47 carrying almost ten times the B-17's fuel load and close to three times that of the B-29. The distinctive swept wings of the B-47 carried six jet engines in a twin and single pod on each side. They could push the B-47E to 606 m.p.h. (Mach 0.84 at 16,300 feet), and the plane could carry two nuclear weapons to a combat radius of over 1,600 miles, and farther with in-flight refueling. Instead of the phalanx of machine guns carried by its predecessors, the B-47 relied primarily on speed for protection, with only a pair of 20-mm cannon in a remote-control tail turret.

B-47s began joining SAC squadrons in 1951, with the ultimate B-47E version making its first flight in 1953. B-47 production totaled 2,060 aircraft, including several hundred EB-47 electronic warfare and RB-47 reconnaissance variants. The B-47 was the most numerous aircraft in SAC during the early 1960s, and was produced in greater numbers than any jet-propelled bomber except possibly its Soviet counterpart, the Tu-16 Badger. In quantity and quality, the B-47 was a milestone in the development of strategic bombers and gave the United States a potent nuclear strike capability.

The Soviets, ever defensively oriented and fully aware of US reliance on nuclear strike aircraft, in the same period revealed a 500 m.p.h. jet fighter-interceptor that could operate at altitudes up to 50,000 feet. This was the MiG-15, a swept-wing fighter that could make bombing missions by the B-36s and B-47s, which flew at lower altitudes, extremely hazardous. Beginning in 1947, some 15,000 to 18,000 MiG-15s were built, more than twice the number of F-86 Sabres (the most numerous Western jet fighter) produced.

This massive deployment of interceptor aircraft—which continues to-

day—was part of the Soviet defensive attitude born of numerous invasions
of what is now the territorial extent of the USSR. In this century, Russia
has been invaded twice by Germany; US, British, French, and Japanese
troops landed in Russia and Siberia to fight the Bolsheviks during the
latter stages of World War I; and there remains (in the Soviet view, at
least) the threat of assault from China in the east and NATO forces in
the west. During the post-World War II period, the threats perceived by
the Soviets—which have perpetuated this defensive attitude—have included US and NATO ground forces, bombers, and missiles, and US
naval forces.

In the immediate postwar era, the US Navy was without a "strategic"
mission in terms of delivering weapons against an enemy's homeland.
The Navy had emerged from World War II as the unquestioned victor
on the seas. No nation, friend or late foe, had warships capable of se-
riously interfering with US use of the sea. The "potential" enemy, the
Soviet Union, had neither a fleet nor a reason to use the sea. Not until
Korea could the US Navy demonstrate that it still was needed in the
atomic age, albeit in support and projection missions (rather than for
control of the sea). If future national strategy was to be based on nuclear
weapons, those in existence were too large for carrier-based planes, let
alone for long-range naval guns, the largest of which was only able to
shoot a projectile 16 inches in diameter some 23 miles.

In searching for a role in the nuclear era, the Navy sought the means
to deliver nuclear weapons against the Soviet Union or other future ene-
mies. Shipboard and submarine test-launchings were conducted with cap-
tured German V-2 rockets and V-1 jet-propelled missiles. These efforts,
however, yielded no practical result until the mid-1950s. More immediately, experiments were undertaken with the P2V Neptune, a twin-
engine, long-range patrol/anti-submarine bomber.[4] P2V Neptunes were
used in test launches from carrier flight decks, and the bomb-bays of
twelve were modified to accommodate nuclear weapons. During a series
of tests in 1948-49, one or two P2V Neptunes would be loaded aboard

---

4. A P2V Neptune held the world's aircraft distance record from 1946 until 1962,
having flown a distance of 11,236 miles from Perth, Australia, to Columbus, Ohio. Also,
an Army Air Forces B-29 flew nonstop from Honolulu over the North Pole to Cairo,
Egypt, a distance of 9,500 miles. However, neither of these flights had any strategic
significance, except for testing flight crew endurance, because the planes carried no
bombload and had no schedule, speed, or altitude demands.

one of the Navy's three large carriers of the *Midway* class at dockside.[5] The ship would steam out to sea and launch the aircraft. After taking off, the Neptunes would fly to a simulated target, pretend to release a nuclear weapon, and then return to a land base. In time of war, either the crew would bail out after releasing the weapon or, if it could be coordinated, the plane would fly out to sea and ditch near a waiting US submarine. This one-way bombing mission was also accepted by the US Air Force as a means for reaching certain Soviet targets in central Asia. Such plans were not officially suicide missions: the crews were instructed to reach a neutral nation or, if necessary, bail out over a remote area of the USSR and await the end of the war (a matter of days, at most).

As previously noted, the Korean War, which began in June 1950, shattered the illusions of the nuclear-capable bomber as the final arbiter of modern war. As late as October 19, 1949, General Omar N. Bradley, Chairman of the US Joint Chiefs of Staff, had addressed the question of conventional-versus-strategic actions in these words:

> I am wondering whether we shall ever have another large-scale amphibious operation. Frankly, the atomic bomb, properly delivered, almost precludes such a possibility.

The Korean War nevertheless included several amphibious landings. (The invasion force at the Inchon landing consisted of a US Marine division, an Army infantry division, and most of a Marine aircraft wing, plus supporting troops, all carried and supported by an armada of over 230 ships.)

During the three years of war on the peninsula, the theater commander, General Douglas MacArthur, asked that nuclear weapons be employed to halt the masses of Chinese "volunteers" that entered North Korea in the winter of 1950-51. President Truman (and other US leaders) were against using nuclear weapons. There was a fear in Washington that American use of nuclear weapons would widen the war, possibly bringing Soviet forces directly into the conflict or precipitating Soviet action in Europe. Other factors included the second use of nuclear weapons against

---

5. The three *Midway*-class aircraft carriers, completed in 1945-47, were the largest ships built during the World War II era except for the two Japanese battleships and one carrier of the *Yamato* class. The *Midway*-class ships displaced 55,000 tons full load, were 986 feet long, and could operate 137 piston-engine carrier aircraft.

an Asian people, the credibility of the war as a United Nations action if a weapon that only the United States possessed were employed, the difficulty of determining targets that warranted the devastation which nuclear weapons would cause, and the possibly limited number of nuclear weapons in the US arsenal. Reportedly, General MacArthur argued for employing between 30 and 50 bombs in Korea—a significant portion of the approximately 400 nuclear weapons available at the time.

During the Korean War, US striking power in Europe was increased against the fear that Korea was merely a Communist diversion in Asia while the main blow was about to fall in Europe. SAC began rotational training flights of squadrons to overseas bases in order to provide forward deployments of bombers. Most of these flights were sent to Britain, but SAC bombers also operated from bases in French Morocco, Libya, Guam, and Japan. (B-29s participating in the Korean War flew from bases in Japan and Okinawa.)

By this time, the US Navy was ready to make an initial contribution to the nation's nuclear strike capability. In February 1951—eight months after the Korean War began—six of the new AJ-1 Savage (piston) and three P2V-3C Neptune (piston) bombers flew across the Atlantic to Port Lyautey, Morocco. Beginning in March 1951, the Savages periodically flew from two of the large *Midway*-class carriers that were then operating in the Mediterranean.

Both of the aircraft carriers had nuclear weapons on board, having been the first ships modified for handling atomic bombs. The Savages could operate from carriers; but the larger Neptunes had to remain ashore because they required dockside loading by large cranes. Thus, if nuclear war appeared "imminent," the Savages would land on the carriers, refuel, load nuclear weapons, and take off when the carriers came within range (1,600 miles on a one-way trip) of Soviet targets. The bombs were assembled aboard the carriers in special, highly restricted spaces by large numbers of technicians who required about 24 hours to put the bombs together. Still, the aircraft carriers were sovereign US territory, fully independent of the complex considerations involved in a nuclear-armed aircraft taking off from a base on foreign soil.

Subsequently, additional aircraft carriers, including the smaller *Essex*-class ships, were fitted to handle nuclear weapons. The AJ Savage and, later, the A3D Skywarrior (jet) attack planes were added to their normal air groups—up to a dozen planes on the larger carriers, and four planes on each of the *Essex*-class ships.

The Korean War was not a Communist diversionary tactic, and no US-Soviet confrontation occurred during the conflict. US military planners did consider using atomic bombs in the Far East during the winter of 1950-51, when Communist Chinese troops threatened to destroy the US ground forces in North Korea, and again in the spring of 1954, when Communist Viet Minh units surrounded a French ground force at Dienbienphu in Indochina. B-29s or B-50s based on American-controlled Okinawa would have been used to strike Chinese troops massing in Manchuria or entering Korea across the Yalu River. The plan for strikes in Indochina presented more complex problems. Initial proposals involved sending large numbers of B-29s from the Philippines or carrier-based planes to pound Viet Minh positions around Dienbienphu with conventional bombs. As the situation worsened for the French, American leaders considered employing nuclear weapons. The sovereignty of the Philippines prevented the loading of nuclear weapons at US bases in that island nation. Okinawa and Guam were too far for effective use of the B-50s. On the other hand, at least two of the US Navy's eight aircraft carriers in the western Pacific had nuclear weapons on board, and the squadron of AJ Savages then in Japan could have been rapidly flown out to the carriers to provide a nuclear strike capability.[6] (See Figure 2-7.)

For a number of reasons, the US government decided against direct intervention in Indochina with either conventional or nuclear bombs. The reasons were similar to those that led to the decision not to use nuclear weapons in Korea. (See Figure 2-8.) Dienbienphu fell in May 1954, and the First Indochina War soon came to an end. Thus, US military planners gave consideration to using nuclear weapons on three occasions during the periods of US monopoly and overwhelming superiority in nuclear weapons: the Berlin crisis of 1948, the Korean War, and Dienbienphu.

During those years, the US nuclear strike capability increased from a handful of bombs deliverable by piston-powered B-29s to—by 1955—some 200 B-36s and over 1,000 B-47s capable of carrying atomic bombs. Added to this force was the Navy's growing carrier-based nuclear strike capability. The Navy had lost out in its effort to construct a huge "su-

---

6. Admiral Arthur D. Radford, at the time Chairman of the US Joint Chiefs of Staff, later informed the author that the carrier-based strike option would have been used if the decision had been made to employ nuclear weapons in Indochina.

percarrier'' in 1949. Secretary of Defense Louis Johnson and, to a lesser extent, General Eisenhower (then President of Columbia University) had the decisive influence on a split Joint Chiefs of Staff with respect to the issue of whether to build the ship or, alternatively, by implication, to emphasize strategic bombers. The Navy continued to argue for a sea-based nuclear strike capability beyond the few AJ Savages aboard its existing carriers. A Navy spokesman contended that ''we cannot safely place reliance on any single weapon or weapon system, but must carry a relatively 'full bag'—must keep them versatile and adaptable to any situation.''

The Korean War demonstrated that the United States would participate in conventional wars, and, significantly, that navies and even aircraft carriers were still needed in the atomic age. A program of large carrier construction was begun, initially at the rate of one supercarrier per year. The first, the USS *Forrestal*, was completed in 1955. The *Forrestal* and later large or ''super'' carriers further increased US forward-deployed nuclear strike capabilities. The backbone of US strategic forces into the 1950s, however, was the bombers of the Strategic Air Command. (See Figure 2-9.)

3

United States Superiority

The US monopoly of nuclear weapons ended in August 1949, when the Soviet Union exploded a fission device. This event was a milestone on the Soviet path to becoming a superpower, and set the stage for a world with two superpowers. It would be several years, however, before the Soviet Union had nuclear weapons in large numbers or the means to deliver them against the United States.

The first Soviet aircraft capable of carrying an atomic bomb was the Tu-4 Bull.[7] Three US B-29 Superfortresses had landed in Soviet Siberia in 1944 after bombing raids against Manchuria and Japan. These aircraft were copied by the Soviets in remarkable time, and the first Tu-4 Bull flew late in 1946. The aircraft was soon in series production, and some 1,200 Bulls were delivered during the next few years. This was how the *Aviatsiya Dalnovo Deistviya*, or Long-Range Aviation (LRA), obtained a "strategic" bomber. With a bomb-load of five and a half tons, the Bull could fly 3,000 miles at a cruising speed of some 225 m.p.h. This meant that by taking off from bases in northern Russia and Siberia, the planes could reach some targets in the northern United States on a 13-hour, one-way flight. The limited number of Soviet bombers available through the 1950s, the duration of their flight, the network of US radar warning

---

7. Tu-4 is the Soviet designation; B-names are US-NATO designations of Soviet bomber aircraft; one-syllable names are for piston aircraft and two-syllable names are for jet aircraft.

stations that stretched across the Canadian Arctic, and the manned interceptor aircraft of the United States and Canada reduced the potential effectiveness of a Soviet nuclear strike capability against the United States during the decade of the 1950s.

But this limited Soviet nuclear strike capability, and the subsequent Soviet explosion of a nuclear fusion device, spurred additional US strategic weapons developments. The United States exploded the first nuclear fusion or thermonuclear device—the precursor of the hydrogen bomb—on November 1, 1952; the Soviets dramatically followed this achievement less than a year later with their first thermonuclear detonation.

Mastery of fusion technology would have far reaching implications in the arithmetic of nuclear arms. The significance of the thermonuclear or hydrogen bomb lies in the enormous energy-releasing efficiency of fusion as compared with fission. Whereas fission weapons were measured in terms of kilotons (KT), or thousands of tons of TNT equivalency, fusion weapons were discussed in terms of megatons (MT), or millions of tons of TNT equivalent. A one-megaton thermonuclear warhead possesses about 50 times the explosive power of the A-bombs used at Nagasaki, but weighs only half as much and is more compact.[8] This meant that when H-bombs became available in the mid-1950s, one large bomber could deliver four weapons with a combined megatonnage equivalent to three hundred bombs of the size dropped on Japan.[9]

The advent of smaller fission and fusion weapons led to the development of US Air Force and Navy fighter/attack-type aircraft that could deliver "tactical" nuclear weapons. By 1952 the Mk 5 nuclear bomb weighing 3,000 pounds and the Mk 8 weighing 3,300 pounds were available. These were a third the size of the smallest bombs previously produced.

In the Air Force, the new, smaller nuclear-capable aircraft began with the F-100 Super Sabre "fighter," while the Navy's first new nuclear plane was the diminutive (11-ton gross weight) A4D Skyhawk. Although these fighter/attack aircraft were considered as "tactical" in US military semantics, an F-100 based in West Germany or an A4D aboard an aircraft carrier in the eastern Mediterranean could deliver a nuclear weapon

---

8. One megaton (MT) is the explosive equivalent of one million tons of TNT, or one thousand kilotons (KT).

9. Based on unofficial estimates that a US B-52 bomber can carry four Mk 28 weapons of about one and a half megatons in its bomb-bay.

against cities in the USSR, thus blurring clear distinctions between tactical and strategic nuclear delivery systems.

Possibly more significant on a long-term basis, the advent of small nuclear warheads meant that the delivery of weapons of mass destruction would become feasible with unmanned missiles. In the United States, this potential was partially fulfilled with the development and limited deployment of low-altitude, air-breathing "cruise" or guided missiles.[10] This concept was an outgrowth of the German V-1 or "buzz bomb," with the missiles following a preset flight path to a fixed target; the lack of terminal accuracy in these weapons was compensated for by the high destructive force of the nuclear warhead.

These cruise missiles included the Air Force's Matador, with a 600-nautical mile range (which was renamed Mace in later variants, with a range of 1,200 nautical miles in the final Mace-B missile), and Snark, with a 5,000 nautical mile range; and the Navy's submarine-launched Regulus-I missile, with a range of 500 nautical miles.[11] (See Figures 3-1 and 3-2.) The Matador/Mace missiles were forward-based in Europe and the western Pacific, while the limited number of Snark missiles procured were based briefly at Presque Isle, Maine. The Navy adapted two World War II-built submarines to carry two Regulus missiles each and then built three additional submarines, one of which was nuclear-powered, to carry four or five missiles. With only one or two submarines (four or five missiles) at sea at any given time, however, the Navy's Regulus force added comparatively little megatonnage to the nation's nuclear striking forces.

The development of small nuclear warheads also permitted the US Army to deploy tactical nuclear weapons. These included nuclear rounds for 280-mm and 8-inch (203-mm) guns, the Honest John and Redstone battlefield missiles, and atomic demolitions—"mines"—that could be emplaced along probable Soviet routes of advance through West Germany. Army interest in nuclear weapons predated battlefield use, however, as evidenced by the Jupiter Intermediate Range Ballistic Missile (IRBM).[12] This was a true rocket missile, developed, like the Redstone,

---

10. Cruise or guided missiles have a variable, aerodynamic flight characteristic whereas ballistic missiles have essentially a fixed, ballistic trajectory.

11. All missile ranges are given in nautical miles (1.15 statute miles).

12. ICBM ranges are defined as 3,000 to 8,000 nautical miles; IRBM ranges as 1,500 to 3,000 miles; and MRBM (Medium Range Ballistic Missile) ranges as 600 to 1,500 miles.

with the help of Werner von Braun and other former German missile scientists. The Jupiter, with a range of 1,500 miles, was intended for basing in NATO nations for strikes against the Soviet Union; it was a true strategic weapon. Simultaneously, the US Air Force was also developing an interest in ballistic missiles, and initiated the Thor IRBM (1,500 miles) and the Atlas and Titan Intercontinental Ballistic Missiles (ICBMs), with initial ranges of 5,500 and 6,300 miles, respectively. (See Figure 3-3.) Interservice rivalry soon led to the decision that the Air Force would operate all IRBMs and ICBMs. The first six Atlas ICBMs became operational in 1959 in the United States, while the Thor IRBMs were installed in Great Britain under joint UK-US control, and subsequently the Jupiter IRBMs were planned for deployment in Greece and Turkey.

In retrospect, the decision to assign IRBMs to the Air Force, which already was directing development of the longer-range ICBMs, cannot be argued. The IRBM and ICBM missions were congruent. Although submarine-based strategic missiles have the same mission as IRBMs and ICBMs, the nature of the submarine platform with respect to equipment, operation, training, support, and other considerations so far has appeared to warrant the operation of these missiles by the Navy, rather than the Air Force or a separate strategic missile force. With the reallocation of military missile roles, the Defense Department established the Advanced Research Project Agency (ARPA) on February 7, 1958, to manage US space programs.[13] Under ARPA's auspices, the nation's nonmilitary space programs were pushed forward, and on July 16, 1958, the Congress passed legislation leading to the establishment of the National Aeronautics and Space Administration (NASA) to manage the nation's nonmilitary space activities. ARPA continues to pursue advanced-technology programs for military use.

Emphasis on Bombers

Despite the variety of cruise and ballistic missiles put forward by the US services during the 1950s, primary US attention was focused on strategic bombers. The Navy operated 14 to 16 attack carriers in the post-Korea period, each provided with 50 or more nuclear strike aircraft: up

---

13. ARPA was subsequently redesignated the Defense Advanced Research Project Agency (DARPA) to better indicate the fact that it is an agency of the Department of Defense.

to one squadron of the large A3D Skywarrior or later the A3J Vigilante, plus A4D Skyhawk bombers. For a brief period apparently some carrier fighter aircraft were also equipped to deliver nuclear weapons. During periods of crisis, the carriers in the Mediterranean and western Pacific would off-load their fighters and embark additional strike aircraft. For example, in 1960-61 the carrier *Coral Sea* operated in the western Pacific with 83 attack aircraft capable of delivering nuclear weapons (plus three electronic aircraft and one cargo aircraft).

The US Air Force reached a peak strategic bomber strength in 1959 with 1,366 B-47s and 488 B-52s, in addition to 174 RB-47 reconnaissance aircraft, which were serviced by over 1,000 KC-97 and KC-135 tanker aircraft. These SAC bombers were the mainstay of US strategic forces, and the nation's available cruise and ballistic missiles and carrier-based bombers paled in comparisons of numbers and megatonnage. For example, the six Atlas-D missiles operational at the end of 1959 could each lift an estimated three-megaton warhead, which in total constituted only half the megatonnage that a single B-52 could deliver carrying bombs and short-range nuclear attack missiles.

Through 1957, US production lines produced 2,040 B-47s. These planes, in the strike configuration, could deliver one to two nuclear weapons and had a maximum range of 4,000 miles. Based overseas and requiring in-flight refueling, they could reach Soviet targets and then either fly on to neutral territory or return to base. Beginning in June 1955, the Strategic Air Command received the larger, eight-jet B-52. (See Figure 3-4.) This aircraft, which first flew in 1952, would become the "ultimate" strategic bomber produced in quantity by the United States. The B-52 could carry four H-bombs some 5,000 miles, hit a target, and return to base without refueling. After the loss of a U-2 reconnaissance aircraft on May 1, 1960, however, Soviet missiles forced a change in US strategic bomber tactics to low-level flights. This considerably reduced their effective range. Maximum speed of this eight-engine giant is 600 m.p.h. B-52 production had run to 699 aircraft when deliveries stopped late in 1962.

Two subsequent strategic bomber programs were initiated in the 1950s, the B-58 Hustler and B-70 Valkyrie. (See Figure 3-5.) The B-58, which flew in 1956, was a "small" aircraft (160,000 pounds gross compared to 488,000 pounds for the later model B-52s) designed to streak over targets at twice the speed of sound. A sleek-looking plane with four jet pods slung under a delta wing, the B-58 had a limited range, and only 104 aircraft were built, including some configured as TB-58 trainers. The B-70 program was essentially stillborn. This aircraft, which was to have been the successor to the B-52, was a giant (500,000 pounds gross) six-jet bomber with intercontinental ranges and a service altitude of over 70,000 feet. Top speed was to be more than three times the speed of sound (over 2,000 m.p.h.). The B-70 aircraft was cancelled in 1961 by the incoming Kennedy Administration, which preferred to stress the development of strategic missiles as against bombers, citing the B-70 as being "unnecessary and economically unjustifiable." In addition, the high-flying B-70 would be vulnerable to the advanced anti-aircraft missiles being deployed by the Soviets. Only three XB-70 aircraft were produced for research purposes.

A primary factor in the demise of the B-70 was the increasing bomber defense capabilities of the Soviet Union. US concern for Soviet offensive and defensive capabilities in the late 1950s led to several changes in US strategic force procedures. Soviet air defenses improved to the point that SAC and the Navy were obliged to revise bombing procedures in order to provide for low-level attacks where they would be less vulnerable to Soviet radar detection and interception. This was the period of major Soviet reorganization for defense of the homeland and the development of advanced air defense weapons. (See Chapter 4.) The latter included new fighter-interceptor aircraft, ground radar warning and intercept control stations, and the installation of Surface-to-Air Missiles (SAMs). A Soviet SAM-2 missile shot down Francis Gary Powers' U-2 reconnaissance aircraft high over Sverdlovsk on May 1, 1960, marking the end of several years of US "spy" flights over the Soviet Union. (See Figure 3-6.)

Soviet efforts to develop and deploy advanced air defense weapons, again reflecting the traditional Russian emphasis on defense, required US nuclear strike aircraft to shift plans from high-level attacks to low-level strikes. This tactic could reduce the probability of detection and interception, but also would greatly increase aircraft fuel consumption and increase the stress placed on the aircraft structure. In 1958, SAC also began an "airborne alert" on a test basis, always keeping a few nuclear-armed aircraft in flight to reduce their vulnerability to attack while on the ground and to reduce flight time to targets. The SAC Commander-in-Chief, General Thomas S. Power, told Congress that:

Figure 1-1. This was Hiroshima after suffering history's first atomic bomb attack. Destruction was almost total because of the light building materials used by the Japanese, the absence of an effective civil defense program, and the lack of warning. Note the still-standing concrete structures. (U.S. Navy)

Figure 1-2, Figure 1-3. ''Little Boy'' and ''Fat Man'' were the nuclear weapons exploded over Hiroshima and Nagasaki, respectively. ''Little Boy'' weighed 8,900 pounds, was 120 inches long, 28 inches in diameter, and had an explosive force of 13-KT. The 10,800-pound ''Fat Man'' was 128 inches long, 60 inches in diameter, and had a 23-KT yield. (U.S. Air Force)

Figure 2-1. The B-29 Superfortress was the first nuclear delivery aircraft. Although the United States had some 3,000 B-29s when World War II ended, very few were configured to carry nuclear weapons and there were still fewer nuclear weapons. (A total of 3,960 B- 29s were built; almost that many were additionally cancelled when the war ended.) (Boeing)

Figure 2-2. The Convair B-36 was large and controversial. It was initially designed and ordered late in 1941, to provide a transocean bomber should Great Britain fall to the Germans. When it became operational a decade later the B-36 was vulnerable to contemporary piston and jet-propelled fighter aircraft. (U.S. Air Force)

Figure 2-3. Several schemes were evaluated to provide fighter escort to accompany strategic bombers. One scheme provided for small fighters to be carried in the bombers. Here an F-85 Parisite fighter is being lowered from a modified B-29 in a test launching. The concept never reached operational status except in the prewar U.S. Navy airships *Akron* and *Macon,* which did carry fighter aircraft. (U.S. Navy)

Figure 2-4. Shown here is the B-36 production line at the Fort Worth division of Consolidated Vultee Aircraft Corporation (later Convair Division of General Dynamics). Note the twin jet engines under the port wing of the first aircraft, and the twin 20-mm cannon in the nose. This production bay was 200 feet wide; these B-36D aircraft had a wingspan of 230 feet, hence they are turned at an angle. (Convair)

Figure 2-5. Sleek and fast, the Boeing B-47 Stratojet was the first jet-propelled "strategic" bomber to be flown in large numbers by the United States. Although the plane was limited in range, in-flight refueling and overseas bases—plus one-way missions against some targets—made the B-47 an effective strategic bomber. This is an early B-47A model. (Boeing)

Figure 2-6. A B-47 refuels from a KC-97A tanker aircraft. Although in-flight refueling was developed and evaluated for military as well as civilian aviation before World War II, the gas-hungry strategic bombers led to the deployment of large aerial tanker forces in the postwar era. (Boeing)

Figure 2-7. The North American AJ-1 Savage was the first carrier-based aircraft capable of delivering a nuclear weapon. Propelled by two piston engines with a jet booster in the fuselage, the Savage took up a lot of space. Here 11 Savages fill the forward flight deck of the carrier *Coral Sea*. (U.S. Navy)

Figure 2-8. Despite a limited nuclear capability, the United States fought the Korean War as a conventional, World War II-style conflict. B-29s such as those shown here flew tactical missions over North Korea after the few strategic targets were destroyed in the early days of U.S. air action over the North. Fifteen years later strategic bombers would again be used in a tactical strike role in Asia. (U.S. Air Force)

Figure 2-9. Several strategic bomber designs were flown in prototype stage, among them the U.S. Air Force YB-49 Flying Wing. The Northrop-built bomber had eight jet engines which could push it to 520 mph. The aircraft was too radical for its time, and after extensive testing the concept was discarded. (U.S. Air Force)

Figure 3-1. The SM-62 Snark was an intercontinental guided or cruise missile deployed briefly in the strategic role by the U.S. Air Force. Secretary of Defense McNamara would later cancel the Snark program as well as future manned bomber development in favor of intercontinental ballistic missiles. (U.S. Air Force)

Figure 3-2. The U.S. Navy missile submarine *Grayback* poses with a Regulus-I missile on its launcher while entering San Diego harbor. The *Grayback* was one of five U.S. submarines that were operationally deployed with the Regulus targeted against Soviet Siberia from the late 1950s until 1964. She could carry four Regulus-I missiles in the two hangars faired into her bow. (U.S. Navy)

Figure 3-3. Ice falls from an SM-65 Atlas missile during a launch from Cape Canaveral, Florida (later Cape Kennedy). The ice was formed by topping off the liquid-oxygen fuel. Flames sprout from the approximately 360,000 pounds of thrust developed during liftoff. (U.S. Air Force)

Figure 3-4. A B-52C Stratofortress flies high above the earth on a training mission. Note the eight jet engines in twin underwing pods; auxiliary fuel tanks on outer wings; tail gun position; and tall tail fin. Until the Reagan Administration's emphasis on strategic weapon development in the early 1980s, it seemed likely that the B-52 would be America's last intercontinental bomber. (Boeing)

Figure 3-5. The ultimate American high-altitude strategic bomber was the B-70 Valkyrie, shown here on a test flight in 1965 with a B-58 chase plane. The B-58 represented an effort to develop a small strategic bomber, but was never popular with the SAC leadership. (U.S. Air Force)

Figure 3-6. Shown here are Soviet SA-2 anti-aircraft missiles, given the NATO code name Guideline, on trucks being prepared for a Moscow parade. The white-wall tires indicate these are not operational trucks or missiles. The Soviets used SA-2 missiles to down the U-2 flown by Francis Gary Powers after it lost altitude because of an engine flameout.

Figure 4-1. Another sleek-looking and long-serving product of the Tupolev design bureau is the Tu-16 Badger, a twin-jet aircraft that is in wide use with Soviet Long-Range Aviation and Soviet Naval Aviation. This Badger-D, with a nose radome, is employed in long-range reconnaissance. Most Badgers have glazed "bombardier" noses. Note the tail gun position. (U.S. Navy)

Figure 4-2. A Tu-16 Badger-G is serviced at a Soviet base. The G variant carries air-to-surface missiles. There is a radome under the fuselage, just behind the glazed nose. Although the U.S. Air Force discarded all B-47s during the 1960s, the Badger remains in Soviet LRA and naval service in large numbers.

Figure 4-3. The classic Bear: The Tu-20/Tu-95 Bear is the world's only turboprop strategic bomber aircraft. It has been in first-line service with Soviet Long-Range Aviation (LRA) for more than 25 years. It is flown by the Soviet Navy only in the reconnaissance/ missile-targeting and anti-submarine roles. This Navy-flown Bear-D is being "escorted" by a U.S. Navy F-4 Phantom. (U.S. Navy)

Figure 4-4. An AS-3 air-to-surface missile has just been released by the LRA Bear-C in this photo taken from a Soviet film. The AS-3 or Kangaroo missile resembles an unmanned fighter aircraft, being 49 feet long and weighing some 22,000 pounds. Missile stand-off range with a nuclear warhead was about 400 miles.

Figure 4-5. A Soviet Golf-class strategic missile submarine on the surface. The diesel-electric Golf was the world's first built-for-the-purpose ballistic missile submarine. The lengthened sail structure houses three short-range missiles. (U.S. Navy)

Figure 4-6. This is a closeup of the sail of a Zulu-V submarine, with the structure lengthened to accommodate two SS-N-4 missiles (note missile hatch covers to left). These early Soviet missile submarines had to surface to launch. (U.S. Navy)

Figure 4-7. Submarine-launched SS-N-4 Sark missiles on parade in Moscow during a celebration of the Russian revolution. This missile was replaced aboard the nine Hotel-class nuclear submarines and several Golf-class diesel submarines by the improved SS-N-5 Serb. The latter missile had a greater range and could be launched underwater.

Figure 4-8. A flat-nosed Thor intermediate-range missile is readied for a test launch at Cape Canaveral. Designated SM-75 by the U.S. Air Force, the missile was briefly deployed in Great Britain under joint Royal Air Force-U.S. Air Force control. The 60 missiles were dismantled shortly after the autumn 1962 Cuban missile crisis. (U.S. Air Force)

Figure 4-9. A U.S. Polaris missile submarine awaits its "teeth." This unusual photograph shows the submarine *Sam Rayburn* with its 16 missile tubes open; each can hold an SLBM some 30 feet long. The U.S. Navy built 41 of these large missile submarines between 1959 and 1967. In 1967 the Soviet Union launched its first modern (i.e., 16-tube) SLBM submarine. (U.S. Navy)

We in Strategic Air Command have developed a system known as airborne alert, where we maintain airplanes in the air 24 hours a day, loaded with bombs, on station, ready to go to the target....I feel strongly that we must get on with this airborne alert....We must impress Mr. Khrushchev that we have it, and that he cannot strike this country with impunity.

4

Soviet Nuclear Forces

Soviet nuclear forces followed a course of development somewhat different from that of the United States. At first glance, the Soviets did appear to be following the United States when they copied the B-29 in the Tu-4 Bull aircraft. Previously Soviet long-range bomber development had lagged behind that of the West. Immediately prior to World War I the Russians had built the world's first four-engine aircraft, and during the 1914-18 war 79 of the Sikorsky *Ilya Mourometz* four-engine bombers were built. These giant biplanes set a number of flight records, and in the bomber role had an endurance of four to five hours (maximum speed was 60 m.p.h.) and could deliver over a thousand pounds of bombs.

After the Russian revolutions and Civil War the nation's aviation industry and aircraft technology were given high priority by Stalin. However, the emphasis was on fighter and then ground-attack aircraft. The only four-engine combat aircraft of significance were some 800 Tupolev ANT-6 bombers built in the early 1930s and the Tupolev/Petlyakov Pe-8, of which about 80 were delivered from 1940 onward. Some ANT-6 aircraft were employed as bombers after Germany invaded Russia in June 1941, but most saw service as transports. Even the newer Pe-8 bombers saw only limited service as the shorter-range, single- and twin-engine bombers were emphasized.

The Tu-4 Bull (*nee* B-29) marked a significant increase in capability for Soviet Long-Range Aviation, and more than 1,500 of these aircraft were produced through 1954. Although the Tu-4 could carry the atomic bombs that were available in the USSR in the early 1950s, the planes probably were intended primarily for Eurasian strikes rather than for the almost-impossible raids against the United States.

In the mid-1950s, the West obtained its first look at Soviet jet-era strategic bombers at the annual Moscow air demonstrations. Probably first on the scene was the Tu-16 Badger, a swept-wing bomber comparable in size, role, and performance to the American B-47. (See Figures 4-1 and 4-2.) The Badger has only two engines, each developing an estimated 19,180 pounds of thrust, as compared to 7,200 pounds of thrust for each of six engines in the B-47E— a manifestation of the Soviet tendency to "build big." First flown in 1952 (five years after the B-47), the Badger began entering service with Soviet Long-Range Aviation (LRA) in 1954-55. It could carry a bomb load of three and a half tons for a distance of 3,800 miles, meaning that Badgers could reach many cities in the United States on one-way flights from northern Soviet bases. This would be a seven-hour flight at cruise speeds, still a long flight but more practical than the over 13-hour flight of the piston-engine Tu-4 Bulls. Top speed of the Badger is about 620 m.p.h., slightly faster than the B-47.

A short time later, the Tu-20 Bear bomber appeared.[14] (See Figures 4-3 and 4-4.) First observed in 1955, the Bear is the world's only turbo-prop strategic bomber. It is powered by four large turbo-prop engines mounted on swept wings, each having two contra-rotating propellers. The Bear can reach a maximum speed of 550 m.p.h., and can carry a 12-ton bombload to targets 3,000 to 4,000 miles away and return to base.

Soviet LRA regiments began receiving Bear bombers in 1956-57, and by the end of the decade some 150 Bears and well over 1,000 Badgers were in service. (Total production was approximately 300 Bears and 1,500 to 2,000 Badgers, with many of these Bears and 500 Badgers later being transferred to the Soviet Navy's air arm.) The combined payload of the LRA Bear and Badger force probably totaled no more than 10,000 megatons, a fraction of the estimated 25,000 to 60,000 megatons carried by the US bombers flown by SAC and the Navy.

Soviet industry produced other strategic bombers in this period, notably the four-jet Mya-4 Bison. Like the Tu-20 Bear, however, this aircraft was of limited usefulness in the strategic bombing role because of slow

---

14. The Soviet military designation for this aircraft is Tu-20. US publications generally identify the Bear as the Tu-95, which is the Tupelov design bureau designation.

aircraft speed, the long intercontinental flight distances to US targets, and the need to overfly Canada, where warning and intercept installations were based. Most of the 200 to 300 Bisons produced were rapidly adapted to tanker, photographic, or electronic-reconnaissance roles.

The failure of even such renowned Soviet aircraft designers as Myasishchev and Tupolev to produce suitable strategic bombers is recorded in Party Chairman Khrushchev's purported memoirs, entitled *Khrushchev Remembers*:[15]

> This plane [Mya-4] failed to satisfy our requirements. It could reach the United States, but it couldn't come back....
>
> There were other problems with the Mya-4. We weren't sure it could fly through defense antiaircraft fire. Nor did it perform very well in its flight tests. A number of test pilots were killed. As a result, our fliers didn't have much confidence in it. In the end, we decided to scrap the whole project because it was costing us too much money and contributing nothing to our security.
>
> ***
>
> Later Tupolev built the Tu-95 [Tu-20] turboprop bomber. It could fly no faster than 800 to 850 kilometers per hour nor any higher than 14,000 meters, which was unimpressive even at that time. Admittedly, the Tu-95 had a range of about 12,000 kilometers, which was excellent, but with such a poor cruising speed and altitude that it would be shot down long before it got anywhere near its target. Therefore it couldn't be used as a strategic bomber.

The capabilities of LRA were enhanced somewhat in the mid-1950s as cruise missiles were provided for the Bear and Badger aircraft. These missiles permitted the bombers to "stand-off" from their targets by 100 miles or more and launch nuclear-tipped missiles that would be less vulnerable to interception than the larger bombers. The Soviets favored the use of stand-off weapons—a technique that would increase the attack potential of less-capable planes—to a much greater degree than the US Air Force. The differences in US and Soviet attitudes toward stand-off weapons probably relate to the evolution since the 1920s of differing concepts of strategic bombing. During World War II, the Norden bomb-

---

15. The Khrushchev quotations are from his purported autobiography *Khrushchev Remembers* (Boston: Little, Brown, 1970), and *Khrushchev Remembers—The Last Testament* (Boston: Little, Brown, 1974).

sight was developed for use in B-17 and B-24 bombers to strike specific military and industrial installations in an effort, albeit futile in most instances, to avoid collateral civilian damage. The Soviets did not follow this tradition of strategic bombing; rather, Soviet emphasis on defense bespoke the need to penetrate intensive anti-bomber defenses, which could be better accomplished by a stand-off missile that presents less of a radar target and has a greater speed than a manned bomber.

Missile Development

More significant than the LRA Bears and Badgers were Soviet strategic missile developments. Whereas US strategic bombers could strike the Soviet Union from bases in Europe, North Africa, Guam, and Okinawa, Soviet A-bombers would have a long polar flight across the Arctic regions and Canada before they could reach the United States. As Khrushchev explained:[16]

> Our potential enemy—our principal, our most dangerous enemy—was so far away from us that we couldn't have reached him with our air force. Only by building up a nuclear missile force could we keep the enemy from unleashing war against us.

Geography, the lack of a strategic bomber "tradition," and possibly a Russian ability and propensity to examine alternatives rather than accept "obvious" solutions led to Soviet emphasis on the development of ICBMs in this period. Under Khrushchev's direction, increased resources were allocated to research and development work based on the German V-2 missile. Finally, on August 3, 1957, an SS-6 ICBM rocketed several thousand miles from its launch pad to impact in Soviet Siberia. In guarded words, the Soviet news agency *Tass* announced that a "super-long-distance, intercontinental multistage ballistic rocket flew at an... unprecedented altitude...and landed in the target area." Not for another 16 months would an American Atlas ICBM be tested over its full range.

Barely two months after the first Soviet long-range ICBM test, an SS-6 booster missile carried Sputnik-1—the earth's first artificial satellite—into orbit. This satellite weighed 184 pounds—166 pounds heavier than the first US satellite, which would not be placed into orbit for another

---

16. Ibid.

three months. Further, on November 3, 1957, a month after Sputnik-1, the Soviets launched another satellite, placing the then-phenomenal payload of 1,121 pounds into earth orbit. On board Sputnik-2 was the live dog Layka, instrumented to relay biological data back to earth on the animal's reaction to weightlessness, radiation, and other environmental changes. The satellite Sputnik-3, which was launched into orbit in May 1958, weighed 2,926 pounds, a size not matched by the United States until 1964. These large Soviet satellite payloads could be traded off in early Soviet missiles for greater range or a large warhead; accordingly, when more efficient nuclear warheads became available, advanced Soviet ICBMs could lift much greater explosive loads than their American counterparts.

The early Soviet technological developments that led to these ICBM and satellite accomplishments, and the accompanying advances in nuclear and hydrogen warheads, made it clear that the USSR was embarked on a strategic missile effort far more extensive than that planned by the United States. In February 1956, Soviet Defense chief G. I. Zhukov, addressing the 20th Communist Party Congress in Moscow, had declared that the Soviet armed forces had been "completely transformed" since World War II, and that the USSR already had "diverse atomic and hydrogen weapons, powerful rockets and jet armament of various kinds, including long-range rockets." Although Soviet IRBMs could not reach the United States, such weapons could strike Britain and France. Thus, when Anglo-French forces invaded Egypt in November 1956 in concert with an Israeli assault into the Sinai toward the Suez Canal, the Soviets threatened Britain and France with missile attacks if the invasion were not halted. Even though the Soviet threat came after the Eisenhower Administration had announced its absolute opposition to the Anglo-French assault, the Soviet statement did indicate sufficient confidence to engage in "missile rattling."

The Soviet Navy apparently shared in these early strategic weapon developments. Among the German war material that fell into Soviet hands in 1945 were several submarine-towed containers for V-2 missiles. After being towed underwater to within striking range of an enemy coast, the container was to be ballasted to the vertical position, the missile fueled and checked out, and the missile then fired against the enemy's coastal cities. Although none of these V-2 containers is believed to have become operational in the Soviet Navy, the concept of the Submarine-Launched

Ballistic Missile (SLBM) was clearly recognized by Soviet "techno-crats," and by the early 1950s a major effort was clearly underway to provide the Soviet Navy with an SLBM capability. The first experimental launch of a ballistic missile from a Soviet submarine took place in September 1955. This was four and a half years before the first launchings of US Polaris SLBM test missiles.

During the period 1955-57, seven Soviet diesel submarines were configured with two tubes for the surface launch of the SS-N-4 Sark missile. This weapon had a range of about 300 nautical miles, and could carry a nuclear warhead. These conversions were followed by 23 "Golf" diesel submarines and eight "Hotel" nuclear submarines completed between 1958 and 1962, each of which could fire three of the SS-N-4 Sark missiles.[17] Meanwhile, the first Soviet nuclear submarine went to sea in 1959, less than five years after the USS *Nautilus*. Although all of these submarines were of limited capability in comparison to later US and Soviet ballistic missile undersea craft, they were a clear indication of the direction of strategic weapons development in the USSR. (See Figures 4-5, 4-6, and 4-7.)

Strategic Reorganization

Another aspect of Soviet weapons development and strategy was the reorganizations of the Khrushchev era (from 1953, when he was one of three "coequal" successors to Stalin, to his removal in late 1964). The principal services of the USSR traditionally were the Army and Navy. By the end of World War II, the Soviet Air Forces were firmly established as a separate, albeit secondary, service. The Soviet leadership long had emphasized defense against air attack, and air defense efforts were formalized about 1954 into a separate military service, the *Protivo-voz-dushnoi Oborony Strany* (Air Defense of the Country). Known by its abbreviation PVO, the service controlled Soviet fighter-interceptor aircraft, anti-aircraft guns, surface-to-air missiles, and the related warning and control activities.

The loss of fighter-interceptors to PVO weakened the position of the Soviet Air Forces, as did the vesting of operational control over the

---

17. Postwar Soviet submarine classes are assigned letter code designations by US-NATO intelligence, with the phonetic names "Golf" and "Hotel" being used for the letter "G" and "H" designations, respectively.

Aviatsiya Dalnovo Deistviya (Long-Range Aviation) and the troop-carrying transport aircraft in the Soviet high command. *Morskaya Aviatsiya* (Naval Aviation) remained under total Navy control. Finally, although the Soviet tactical air force, officially known as *Frontovaya Aviatsiya* (Frontal Aviation), is a part of the Air Forces, it operates under the direction of fronts or armies in the battlefield support role.

Khrushchev's interest in the development of intercontinental missiles as the prime striking force of the USSR and his modernization of Soviet strategy led to the establishment in May 1960 of the *Raketnyye Voyska Strategicheskogo Naznacheniya* (Strategic Rocket Forces) as a separate service. The Rocket Forces were given responsibility for the development and operation of all Soviet intermediate and intercontinental-range ballistic missiles. Unlike the US Strategic Air Command, which controls US land-based ICBM and strategic bomber forces, the Soviet Rocket Forces do not control Soviet long-range bombers.

Thus, the USSR has five separate and distinct combat services. In their normal order of listing they are: (1) Strategic Rocket Forces, (2) Air Defense Forces, (3) Ground Forces, (4) Air Forces, and (5) Navy.

The technological advances of the Soviet Union during the latter 1950s did not go unnoticed in the United States. American government and military leaders were faced with two kinds of evidence with respect to Soviet activities. First, there was the verbose bragging of Khrushchev and the "unconfirmed reports" of ominous Soviet military developments. For example, the 1958-59 edition of the annual *Jane's All the World's Aircraft* announced that the Soviets had in operation a six-jet, intercontinental bomber twice as fast as any US bomber then in service. Early in 1959, nuclear experts told Congress that within a year the Soviets would fly a nuclear-powered airplane; a year later, the trade journal *Missiles and Rockets* said that the Soviets were testing a semi-ballistic bomber aircraft with a range of almost 10,000 miles and a maximum speed of almost 14,000 m.p.h.; and press reports of Soviet ICBM tests into the Pacific gave the missiles considerably more accuracy than US weapons. Even the Soviet Navy was being credited with a nuclear strike capability against the United States. One US official estimate declared that Soviet missile submarines would be able to launch a "devastating" attack against the United States "early in the 1960s." The second category of indications consisted of factual evidence regarding Soviet research and experiments in the strategic weapons field. These indications included the development of fission and fusion warheads before Western intelligence services had predicted they would appear.

Soviet developments—real and imagined—led to Senate air power hearings during the spring of 1956 under the gavel of Senator Stuart Symington, who had served as first Secretary of the Air Force. Senior officers of the Air Force testified that there would be a serious "bomber gap" by the early 1960s unless the United States immediately allocated top priority to long-range bomber development. Then came the Soviet ICBM test flights and space spectaculars of 1957, which gave rise to an even more intensive debate which, by the eve of the national election of 1960, became known as the "missile gap" controversy. Once again, US military leaders appeared before Congressional committees to explain the strategic advantages that were accruing to the Soviets through these tests.

The US government initiated counteractions during the late 1950s. A portion of the Strategic Air Command's bombers were placed on airborne alert, orbiting in flight over the United States and ocean areas, ready to attack the USSR when the coded signal was transmitted. Navy carriers in the Mediterranean and western Pacific kept several nuclear-armed aircraft on their flight decks ready for launching. Thor and Jupiter IRBMs were being emplaced in Britain, Italy, and Turkey. (See Figure 4-8.) Further, the US long-range ICBM programs were accelerated, as was development of the Navy's submarine-launched Polaris missile system.

Late in 1955, the Navy had been directed to join the Army in the Jupiter IRBM program, with the goal of placing the 60-foot, liquid-fueled, 1,500-nautical mile missile at sea in submarines. This order was a result of concern over rapid Soviet advances in H-bomb development. Two years later, with smaller warheads and solid propellents becoming feasible for missiles, the Navy dropped from the Jupiter effort and initiated the Polaris SLBM program. (See Figure 4-9.) The original Polaris schedules called for the first missile submarine to be ready for sea in 1963. Concern over Soviet developments led to revisions of schedules and a dramatic intensification of effort, with the result that the first Polaris submarine, the USS *George Washington*, went to sea on its first "deterrent patrol" on November 15, 1960. The nuclear-propelled *George Washington* carried 16 Polaris A-1 missiles armed with nuclear warheads which could be launched from underwater to targets 1,200 miles away. There was a similar acceleration in the development of the longer-range A-2 and A-3 variants of the Polaris missile. (See Figure 4-10.)

Ironically, there was considerable opposition to the Polaris program within the Navy because of fears that (1) the SLBM effort would compete with the Air Force for strategic missions (and, with memories of the Navy defeat in the 1949 carrier-versus-B-36 controversy, there was nothing to be gained from such a dispute), and (2) an accelerated Polaris effort would cost the Navy funds for other programs, especially aircraft carriers. Both fears were justified, although in the long run the Polaris program would be to the Navy's benefit.[18]

When President Kennedy entered the White House in January 1961, the Navy had two Polaris submarines (32 missiles) at sea and 12 others (192 missiles) under construction or fitting out. He immediately ordered five additional submarines, and requested funds from Congress for another ten, to bring the number of such craft built and on order to 29. President Kennedy greatly accelerated US strategic weapons development and deployment, although the numbers of ICBMs, IRBMs, bombers, and SLBMs then in service and on order were already superior to existing Soviet strategic weapons capable of reaching the United States.[19]

18. A comprehensive discussion of these arguments appears in Harvey M. Sapolsky, *The Polaris Systems Development* (Cambridge, Mass.: Harvard University Press, 1972).

19. It soon became evident to those who had access to the intelligence data that a "missile gap" actually existed in favor of the United States, when one considered overall program efforts. In the early 1960s, however, the Soviets were initiating the research and development that would lead to Soviet leadership in several categories of strategic weapons before the decade was over.

5

Confrontation and Restructuring

The "missile gap" that haunted the United States in the late 1950s failed to materialize during the next decade. Despite Khrushchev's directives and bellicose pronouncements, Soviet management and production capabilities were unable to keep pace with the new weapons technologies.

The Soviets suffered major operational and personnel problems. The first Soviet ICBM, the SS-6 Sapwood system,[20] fell short of its range goal and could only reach the United States from launch positions in the northern latitudes, on the Arctic islands of Novaya Zemlya and the Franz Josef groups, and the Arctic mainland at Norilsk and Vorkuta. At those northern latitudes, the climate adversely affected missile reliability and logistics. An advanced Soviet missile engine exploded during a test launch in October 1960, killing the first head of the Strategic Rocket Forces, Marshal Mitrofan Nedelin, and over 300 other observers. This tragedy, as well as other accidents, the problems of training missile officers, and other difficulties of the Soviet strategic weapons programs, have been

---

20. Designations and names for Soviet missiles are US-NATO designations; "S" names indicate surface-to-surface weapons. Of late, only the designations are used.

described by General Staff Colonel-turned-Western spy Oleg Penkovskiy, and by Khrushchev himself.[21]

In an apparent effort to recoup his position in the face of Soviet difficulties and the Western strategic buildup under President Kennedy, Khrushchev made a surprise move during the fall of 1962 by sending Medium-Range Ballistic Missiles (MRBMs) and possibly nuclear-capable bombers to Communist Cuba. Apparently he expected that these weapons, secretly transported to Cuba in merchant ships, could tip the balance of strategic power to the Soviet side. At the least, they could provide a negotiating tool for Khrushchev.

US intelligence detected the Soviet attempt to introduce offensive weapons into Cuba. The Kennedy Administration decided that this situation was unacceptable, and various options were considered for ending the threat of attack from Cuba. These options included destroying the Soviet missiles and bombers by air attack, which proponents acknowledged could not insure total success and would kill Russians; a combined airborne-seaborne assault on the island, which would have led to prolonged and costly ground combat in the island's towns and mountains; or a naval blockade, camouflaged by the expression "quarantine," to halt the further shipment of offensive weapons. The last option, if not successful, still would permit the execution of one or both of the others. Accordingly, on October 22, 1962, President Kennedy announced a 500-mile barrier around Cuba through which no strategic weapons would be permitted to pass. US strategic striking forces were placed on alert, and the White House announced that a Cuban-based attack against any target in the Western Hemisphere would be considered an attack against the United States by the Soviet Union. (See Figures 5-1 and 5-2.)

At the time of confrontation, the United States had several times the long-range strategic weapons and deliverable megatonnage available to the Soviet Union. In addition, the US Navy could, and did, deploy a massive force of general purpose ships—aircraft carriers, cruisers, destroyers, and submarines—in the Caribbean, while the Soviets were unable to project a force of surface warships across the Atlantic to the crisis

---

21. Oleg Penkovskiy, *The Penkovskiy Papers* (New York: Doubleday, 1965), based primarily on the documents sent to the West by Penkovskiy before his exposure and execution by the Soviet Government in 1963. Also see N.S. Khrushchev, *Khrushchev Remembers: The Last Testament.*

area. Still, it was the US arsenal of strategic weapons, tabulated below, that made the Cuban missile crisis a dramatic example of US military superiority.

Excluded from the above comparison of strategic weapons are the IRBMs on Soviet territory that could not reach the United States; the US Thor and Jupiter IRBMs in Britain, Italy, and Turkey, however, could reach Soviet cities. Similarly, while several US Polaris submarines at sea could have fired their weapons against the Soviet Union with only minimal interference from hostile anti-submarine forces, the Soviet SLBM force, consisting of about 30 diesel submarines and several nuclear submarines, was not able to deploy rapidly and cross the Atlantic to bring their short-range (300-nautical mile) missiles into the confrontation. Moreover, US anti-submarine forces were comparatively effective. According to one US admiral: "During the Cuban crisis . . . our ASW forces flushed all [six]

US AND SOVIET STRATEGIC WEAPONS (Fall 1962)

United States	*Soviet Union* *(Approximate)*
639 B-52 heavy jet bombers	100 Tu-20 Bear and Mya-4 Bison heavy bombers[22]
880 B-47 medium jet bombers[23] 76 B-58 medium jet bombers plus carrier-based strike aircraft	1,350 medium jet bombers 42 Il-28 Beagle light jet bombers in Cuba possibly with nuclear capability
142 Atlas ICBMs 62 Titan-I ICBMs 80 Minuteman-I ICBMs	35 SS-6 Sapwood and SS-7 Saddler ICBMs
60 Thor IRBMs 45 Jupiter IRBMs	42 MRBMs being installed in Cuba (42 was the number delivered; sites were being prepared for 48 missiles)
112 Polaris A-1 and A-2 SLBMs in seven nuclear-propelled submarines	

---

22. Additional Mya-4 Bisons served in the reconnaissance and tanker roles.
23. Additional B-47s served in the reconnaissance and electronic warfare roles.

Soviet submarines en route to the Caribbean within a matter of a couple of days from the word 'Go'."

Thus, the United States had strategic superiority. It would be another decade before the Soviet Union could achieve comparable strategic forces. The Soviets withdrew their nuclear-capable missiles and bombers from Cuba. Of course, Cuba remained available as a naval and air base for Soviet "conventional" forces. Apparently, as part of the US-Soviet accord, US-controlled Jupiter missiles were removed from Italy and Turkey. The removal was offset by the almost simultaneous entry of the first Polaris submarine into the Mediterranean in April 1963.

Khrushchev survived the Cuban missile crisis by exactly two years. His ouster as First Secretary of the Communist Party and Prime Minister in mid-October 1964 was due to a number of factors, among them the Soviet backdown in the Cuban missile confrontation. As a reaction to the Kennedy Administration's rapid buildup of US strategic and conventional forces, by late 1961 the Soviet Union had revised its defense programs to further accelerate the production of strategic weapons.

The number of SS-7 Saddler ICBMs, which would become operational sometime in 1962, was increased, and in 1963 the SS-8 Sasin ICBM became operational. Both missiles had storable-liquid fuels and a range in excess of 6,000 nautical miles, and carried five-megaton warheads. By the time of Khrushchev's removal late in 1964, an estimated 200 ICBMs—mostly SS-7 and SS-8 missiles—had been emplaced in the Soviet Union. In this period, too, the Soviets began emplacing missiles in underground silos in an effort to hide them from US overhead (satellite) surveillance, and to increase their survivability in the event of a US preemptive attack.

A succession of new ICBMs entered service with the Soviet Strategic Rocket Forces in the latter 1960s. The huge SS-9 Scarp became operational in 1967, and had a greater payload than any other operational ICBM. (See Figure 5-3.) The SS-9 could deliver a 25-megaton warhead on targets 6,000 nautical miles away. The giant SS-9 soon was employed in the first Soviet tests of multiple-warhead missiles, and then with the Fractional Orbital Bombardment System (FOBS). Under the FOBS concept, the missile is fired in a low trajectory in the opposite direction from the target, enters a partial earth orbit, and then strikes the target. This tactic increases the problems of defending a target, increases the range of the weapon, and provides considerably less warning than an ICBM following a high ballistic trajectory. In this configuration, however, the SS-9 has less accuracy and carries a smaller warhead.

Following the SS-9 into service, the Soviets began deploying the SS-11 in 1966 and the SS-13 in 1969. Both of these ICBMs were smaller weapons. The SS-11, having a storable-liquid propellant, could strike targets in the United States with a one-megaton warhead; the SS-13, which introduced solid-fuel propellant to Soviet ICBMs, has a range of some 5,500 nautical miles, and also carries a one-megaton warhead.

Numerical Advantage

During 1970, the Soviet Union surpassed the United States in numbers of operational ICBMs: over 1,100 Soviet missiles to 1,054 US missiles. Of the former, more than 275 were the large SS-9s, while the number of US large missiles—the Titan-II—remained at 54. In the mid-1960s, moreover, the Soviet Union initiated a major construction program of strategic missile submarines.

The Soviet Navy had completed eight nuclear (Hotel) and 23 diesel (Golf) submarines, each armed with three SLBMs, between 1958 and 1962. In addition, a few older diesel submarines had been converted to fire two of the early missiles. Their limitations have already been described.

The Soviet realignment of strategic weapons that resulted in the creation of the Strategic Rocket Forces in 1960 also led to the Soviet Navy giving up its strategic strike role. Several more planned Hotel and Golf submarines were cancelled, and planning for more advanced SLBM submarines came to a halt. However, the reassessment of the strategic situation in 1961 led to a renewal of interest by the Soviet leadership in the potential effectiveness of submarine-launched strategic missiles. This was reinforced during the Cuban missile crisis, and mass production was initiated of a larger SLBM submarine subsequently assigned the US-NATO code name "Yankee." In 1968, the Soviet Navy completed the first Yankee-class submarine, one year after the US Navy had completed the last of 41 nuclear submarines armed with the Polaris missile. The Yankee is a modern nuclear undersea craft, similar in size to the US Polaris, carrying 16 SLBMs. The initial Yankee SS-N-6 missiles had a range of 1,300 nautical miles, and carried a warhead unofficially estimated at one to two megatons. (In comparison, the initial 1,200-nautical mile Polaris A-1 missile was followed to sea in 1962 by the 1,500-nautical mile A-2 variant, and in 1964 by the 2,500-nautical mile A-3 variant.)

By 1970, there were about ten Yankee-class SLBM submarines (160 missiles) at sea, with annual production estimated at eight submarines a year. US defense officials stated that "as production experience is gained, it is possible that that rate of output . . . will increase significantly. . . . At current construction rates, the Soviets could have from 35 to 50 of the (Yankee) class submarines by 1974-75" (carrying 560 to 800 missiles).

While building up ICBM and SLBM forces during the latter 1960s, the Soviet leadership maintained the level of heavy bombers in Long-Range Aviation, but gradually reduced the medium bomber strength of LRA. In the early 1970s, US defense officials rated LRA at a strength of 150 Bear and Bison bombers, plus 50 Bisons configured as tankers, and over 700 medium bombers. An increasing number of aircraft in both categories were armed with air-to-surface missiles.[24] The Tu-16 Badgers, in service since 1954-55, were joined in the early 1960s by another medium bomber, the Tu-22 Blinder, an aircraft that can reach a maximum speed of 925 m.p.h. (Mach 1.4 at 40,000 ft.) with two turbo-jet engines rated at a phenomenal 26,000 pounds of thrust each. However, whereas the Badger has an unrefuelled range of 3,800 miles with a nuclear weapon, the Blinder's range is only some 2,800 miles, although this can be extended by in-flight refueling. As Soviet ICBM and SLBM forces increased, the medium bomber force of Badgers and Blinders, later supplemented by the supersonic Backfires, continued as a force oriented for operations in the Eurasian theaters and not for strikes against the United States.

A final consideration in the development of Soviet strategic weapons in this period was the cruise missile submarine. As noted earlier, after World War II the US Navy, using German V-1 pulse-jet rocket technology, developed the Regulus submarine-launched cruise missile. This weapon was pursued as a strategic weapon for use against land targets

---

24. From 1960, the AS-3 Kangaroo, with a range of 350 nautical miles; from 1967, the AS-4 Kitchen, with a range of 250 nautical miles; and from 1970, the AS-6, with a range of 300 nautical miles. Under present assumed weapons loadings, US officials estimate that the 150-plane Bear-Bison force can deliver up to 250 nuclear gravity bombs and missiles against the United States in an all-out attack. The number of weapons could be increased severalfold if only nuclear bombs were carried.

because of the lack of hostile surface fleets and the need to compete with the US Air Force for strategic missions.

Building on the same German technology (and, like the US armed services, employing German scientists and technicians), by the mid-1950s the Soviets had undertaken the construction of destroyers and coastal craft armed with anti-ship cruise missiles. Next, several Whiskey-class diesel submarines were converted to fire the large Shaddock SS-N-3 anti-ship missile. This weapon has a high subsonic speed and a maximum range of over 400 nautical miles, and can carry some 2,200 pounds of high explosives or a nuclear warhead in the kiloton range. The initial Whiskey-class conversions carried one or two Shaddocks housed in horizontal cylinders aft of their conning towers. The submarines would surface; the cylinders then elevated and the missiles fired. These conversions were followed by the "long-bin" Whiskey conversions, which had four Shaddock tubes fixed in their conning towers.

After these 13 conversions,[25] the Soviet Navy took delivery of several classes of especially built Shaddock missile submarines: 16 of the diesel Juliett-class, each with four missiles; five Echo-I-class nuclear submarines, each with six missiles; and 29 of the Echo-II-class nuclear submarines armed with eight missiles. Today the Juliett and Echo-II submarines remain in first-line Soviet service, as well as a number of newer submarines armed with shorter-range anti-ship missiles.

Although the Shaddock SS-N-3 missile generally is considered an anti-ship weapon, it could be employed against land targets with a range of at least 400 nautical miles. Some observers contend that the Shaddock was deployed in submarines to provide missile coverage of the southern United States when Soviet land-based missiles and manned bombers could reach only the northern regions of the country. A US Navy presentation to Congress in 1973 noted "we know that [Shaddocks] are tactical cruise missiles. But we also are certain that with a modification, which really involves only the warhead of the missile, the Shaddock would be used to strike targets in the United States." In the same session, Navy officials pointed out that a Shaddock-armed submarine operating 150 nautical

---

25. According to naval reference works, the Soviet Navy converted one single-cylinder Whiskey submarine, five twin-cylinder Whiskey submarines, and seven "long-bin" Whiskey submarines. The six early ships with exposed missile cylinders were extremely noisy because of their awkward configuration and probably were relegated primarily to test and training roles.

miles off the US coast could strike coastal cities and as far inland as Pittsburgh, Atlanta, and Dallas. Shaddock-armed submarines, which have periodically operated in the Caribbean Sea at least since 1970, possess the capability of striking targets in the southern United States. These submarine missiles, with their low flight profile and southerly direction of attack, strain US detection and defense capabilities, and add another dimension to the threat from Soviet strategic weapons.

During the late 1960s, the Soviet strategic forces attained a high rate of deployment, with emphasis on ICBMs and SLBMs; additionally, several of the Shaddock missile submarines possibly were assigned to a strategic strike role. Clearly ICBMs constituted the main Soviet strategic force, followed by the SLBM force. Further, Soviet deployments were in excess of most US intelligence estimates. By the end of 1970 there were some 1,440 operational Soviet ICBM launchers, with at least 17 of the Yankee-class missile submarines operational (carrying a total of 272 missiles). More missile silos were reported to be under construction, although the rate of deployment was decreasing, while another 15 or more Yankee SLBM submarines (with 240 missile tubes) were reported on the building ways or being prepared for service. US intelligence sources also cited as under development an SLBM with a much longer range than the 1,300-nautical-mile SS-N-6 of the Yankee class.

Significantly, the Soviet Union did not improve its long-range bomber force, apparently because of (1) the geographic limitations to direct USSR-to-US bomber strikes, (2) the lack of overseas bases for Soviet bombers and tankers, and (3) the lack of a politically strong air force organization to compete for long-range bomber development.

US Second-Generation Weapons

As the Soviets reached a high rate of ICBM and SLBM deployments in the late 1960s, the US deployment of new strategic weapons ended. The Kennedy Administration, which began in January 1961 in the "missile gap" period, undertook an acceleration of both strategic and conventional warfare programs. Simultaneously, the concept of systems analysis was brought forward to a previously unprecedented degree in an effort to develop the optimum "mix" of strategic forces. The nature of the future strategic mix was discussed in these terms by President Kennedy's Secretary of Defense, Robert S. McNamara:

> The introduction of ballistic missiles is already exerting a major impact on the size, composition, and deployment of the manned bomber force, and this impact will become greater in the years ahead. As the number of . . . ballistic missiles increases, requirements for strategic aircraft will be gradually reduced. Simultaneously, the growing enemy missile capability will make grounded aircraft more vulnerable to sudden attack.

During the early 1960s, the remaining US first-generation ICBMs became operational: the Atlas-E in 1960, the Titan-I in 1962, and the Atlas-F in 1962, all with storable-liquid propellants and capable of reaching the Soviet Union from launching pads in the United States. (See Figure 5-4.)

These weapons were followed into service by the second-generation missiles, the Minuteman-I and the Titan-II. The Minuteman-I (of which two versions were developed simultaneously) had a solid propellant and could deliver a one-megaton warhead against targets 6,300 nautical miles away. This was America's first solid-fuel ICBM. The Minuteman was installed in underground launch silos to provide protection against preemptive enemy missile or bomber attacks on the US deterrent force. Whereas the Minuteman was a "light" ICBM, the Titan-II was the largest US ICBM to be developed, weighing almost five times as much as the Minuteman and carrying a warhead of about nine megatons for a distance of 6,300 nautical miles. This was a storable-liquid missile, intended to be replaced after a few years.

As the Minuteman and Titan programs got under way, their proponents advocated large deployments to insure numerical superiority over Soviet strategic forces. Air Force leaders spoke about up to 2,500 Minuteman ICBMs. Actual planning in the early 1960s called for 1,200 Minuteman missiles and 120 Titan-II weapons as the second-generation SAC missile force. Although Secretary NcNamara favored missiles over bombers, he restricted the numbers of ICBMs deployed to what he considered realistic force levels. In addition, the improved Minuteman-II (first operational in 1966) had increased accuracy over the previous Minuteman missiles. (See Figure 5-5.)

The actual force levels eventually were established at 1,000 Minuteman and 54 Titan missiles. At the same time, Secretary McNamara accelerated the phasing out of the earlier strategic missiles. The Snark long-range cruise missile was discarded in 1961, less than four months after some

30 of these weapons had been declared combat-ready. The exposed Thor IRBMs in Britain, operated jointly by SAC and the Royal Air Force, were discarded in 1963. During the next two years, all of the nation's first-generation ICBMs were phased out: the 30 Atlas-D, 33 Atlas-E, 80 Atlas-F, and 63 Titan-I missiles. These actions led to the stabilization of the ICBM force at 1,000 Minuteman and 54 Titan missiles in the mid-1960s, the number of ICBMs that would be in the SAC inventory for the next two decades. These weapons were to undergo significant qualitative improvements, which will be discussed in the next chapter.

With respect to manned strategic bombers, the Kennedy Administration began phasing out the entire B-47 medium bomber force. SAC jet bomber strength reached a peak of 1,854 aircraft in late 1959: 488 of the intercontinental B-52s, and the remainder medium-range B-47s. The phaseout of older B-47s actually began in 1959, and was accelerated after the Kennedy Administration took office in January 1961. The Berlin crisis of 1961 and the Cuban crisis of 1962 briefly delayed the B-47 phaseout, and the deliveries of B-52 and B-58 jet bombers also briefly offset the B-47 reductions.

The strike capabilities of the B-52 aircraft were improved beginning in 1961 when the Hound Dog air-to-ground missile and the Quail decoy missile became operational. A B-52 could carry two Hound Dog missiles under each wing. These turbojet missiles have a maximum speed of over Mach 2 and a maximum range of over 500 miles for attacking enemy defenses or heavily defended targets. Each Hound Dog has a warhead of about one-megaton. The Quail decoy, carried in the rear bomb-bay of a B-52, is also turbojet-powered; it has a high subsonic speed and a range of over 200 miles. The Hound Dogs were intended to destroy hostile missile defenses and the Quails were to be released by B-52s to simulate bomber images on enemy radars. These missiles would help the bombers penetrate to their targets to release ''gravity'' bombs.

The last B-52s and B-58s were delivered to SAC in 1962, and for the first time since 1946 there were no strategic bomber aircraft being developed or produced in the United States. SAC bomber strength fell to 591 B-52s and 83 B-58s in late 1966, when the last B-47 bombers were retired (although 16 reconnaissance-version RB-47s were retained for a few months longer). Meanwhile, phaseout of the B-58s had begun, and all of those high-speed, short-range aircraft were gone by 1970. Curtis E. LeMay, the ''father of SAC,'' and many other Air Force generals felt that the B-58 was too small and short-legged to be an effective strategic bomber. Also, because only 116 were built (including 30 prototype and service test aircraft), the B-58 was relatively expensive to support.

As the number of manned bombers declined, the expensive airborne alert program was also cancelled. The increasing number of dispersed Minuteman ICBMs in underground silos, the large Polaris submarine force, and the completion of early warning systems that could provide at least 15 minutes warning of a Soviet missile attack alleviated the need for the airborne alert. Instead a large percentage of the planes were kept on 15-minute runway alert.

Also during the 1960s, these large strategic aircraft were employed in a conventional warfare role against Viet Cong positions in South Vietnamese jungles. On June 18, 1965, 27 B-52F bombers flying from Guam initiated strategic bomber participation in the Vietnam War. Subsequent B-52 raids conducted during the next seven years were considered effective in support of ground operations. The giant bombers were undetectable by Viet Cong troops in South Vietnam until their bombs were falling. Thus, the older B-52 aircraft were committed to the Vietnam War in a tactical role.

Operating from Guam and then bases in Thailand, the B-52s suffered several operational losses as they pounded suspected Viet Cong positions in South Vietnam. Then, as part of President Nixon's efforts to force the Communists into meaningful negotiations, on April 17, 1972 the giant B-52s made their first attack against the North Vietnamese cities of Hanoi and Haiphong. This raid stirred a storm of controversy in the United States over the issue of war escalation, but the B-52s continued to strike specific targets near the North Vietnamese capital into early 1973. During the B-52 strikes 17 of the aircraft were lost over North Vietnam, all but two during the eleven-day period December 18-28.

Bombing with conventional weapons from high altitudes and flying predictable approach routes, the B-52s were vulnerable to the heavy surface-to-air missile defenses and MiG fighters. The losses would have been higher had the B-52 missions not been coordinated with tactical Air Force and Navy strikes, screened by protective fighters, and preceeded to the targets by electronic jamming aircraft. (None of these protective measures would be available in a strategic attack against the Soviet Union; however, it is expected that the bombing tactics, nuclear weapons, decoys, and coordination with ICBM and SLBM attacks would serve to increase the survivability of the B-52s to the Soviet targets.)

During the Vietnam War period (1964-72), the overall B-52 force was reduced from some 625 aircraft to 450, although there were some qualitative improvements to the bombers through modernization. In the midst of this bomber drawdown, Secretary McNamara suddenly introduced a new "strategic" manned bomber, the FB-111. Immediately after the last B-52 and B-58 bombers were delivered to SAC in 1962, Secretary McNamara had requested the Air Force to "consider an alternative bombing system" as a follow-on to the B-52, B-58, and B-70 manned bombers. This would be an aircraft that could launch long-range, stand-off strategic missiles, and thus would not have to penetrate the increasing Soviet air defenses. By the early 1960s, Soviet air defenses included over 4,000 jet interceptor aircraft and almost 8,000 surface-to-air missiles, with an on-going modernization program.

Then, two days after an announcement of further reductions of the SAC bomber force, on December 8, 1965, Secretary McNamara announced that the controversial swing-wing TFX "fighter" would be procured by SAC as a follow-on manned bomber. He directed that 210 aircraft be built in the FB-111 bomber variant.[26] The FB-111, like the B-58 Hustler and B-52 Stratofortress, would have to penetrate Soviet air defenses. In the event, only 76 of the FB-111 strategic bombers were built to equip four SAC squadrons, which currently fly 66 of the FB-111A aircraft.

The Strategic TRIAD

The third major US strategic system developed during the 1960s was the Polaris Submarine-Launched Ballistic Missile (SLBM) fleet. Together with land-based ICBMs and manned bombers, the Polaris submarines were considered the "third leg" of what became known about 1970 as TRIAD.

Although the Navy was initially opposed to large-scale Polaris devel-

---

26. Early estimates of the F-111 program provided for some 1,700 aircraft to be used by the US Air Force, Navy, and Marine Corps, and Australia and Great Britain. Because of subsequent dissatisfaction with the aircraft in some quarters, as well as budgetary constraints, only 442 were acquired by the US Air Force in the F-111 fighter variants through 1974, plus 76 FB-111 strategic bombers, and 24 aircraft for Australia. Adding in the few planes produced for the cancelled US Navy and British programs, the total F-111/FB-111 program through 1974 was approximately 550 aircraft.

opment, a forceful Chief of Naval Operations, Admiral Arleigh A. Burke, and his full endorsement of the project manager, Rear Admiral W. F. Raborn, got Polaris to sea far in advance of early schedules. By the early 1960s, the Navy was planning a 45-submarine force (five squadrons of nine submarines each). Secretary McNamara, however, cut the planned force to 41 submarines (656 missiles), and the last Polaris submarine went to sea in April 1967, seven and a half years after the first. (Thirteen nuclear-propelled Polaris submarines were commissioned in the peak year of 1964, about the same number of Yankees completed in the peak year of the Soviet Yankee-class SLBM program.)

In the early 1960s, as the Polaris submarines joined the fleet, the Navy's 15 attack aircraft carriers were relieved of their primary nuclear strike role. The aircraft carriers do retain a nuclear strike capability, however, and continue to be a part of the nuclear attack plans. (See Figure 5-6.)

The components of the US strategic offensive force developed during the 1960s, with differing origins, effectiveness, and operational concepts, became linked together by the term TRIAD—after the fact of their existence. The decisions of the 1960s with respect to numbers of platforms would dictate the size of US strategic offensive forces into the 1980s: 1,054 ICBMs, approximately 450 manned bombers, and 41 submarines with 656 missiles. In addition, forward-based tactical aircraft in Europe and forward-deployed aircraft carriers could reach the USSR with "tactical" nuclear weapons. While the size of the US strategic offensive force in the 1970s was shaped by the deployments of the previous decade, Soviet strategic weapon deployments were continuing into the 1970s, and both superpowers soon would introduce new strategic weapons technologies.

6

Offense Versus Defense

During the 1960s, two aspects of strategic weapons began to dominate the arms race: ballistic missile defense and multiple warheads. The two issues are closely related in that each of these is in part a counter to the other. Before examining the chronology of events surrounding these concepts, it may be useful to examine the concepts themselves as dominant factors in strategic weapons development.

With the proliferation of ICBMs by the United States and Soviet Union in the 1960s, the amount of destruction that each side could inflict became enormous. Both superpowers had large proportions of their population and industrial capacity concentrated in cities. According to statements by Secretary of Defense McNamara, the destruction of 200 American cities could kill over half of the nation's population and eliminate three quarters of its industrial capacity, while the loss of 400 Soviet cities would mean that almost half of that nation's population and three quarters of its industry could be destroyed.

At the same time, technologies were becoming available that gave promise of an active ballistic missile defense whereby incoming ICBM warheads could be intercepted with Anti-Ballistic Missile (ABM) missiles. An active missile defense system consists principally of radars to detect and track incoming Reentry Vehicles (RVs), and interceptor missiles to destroy these RVs. Formal US efforts to develop an ABM system began with the Army's Nike-Zeus system, initiated in 1956. Such a

DISTRIBUTION OF POPULATION AND
INDUSTRIAL CAPACITY (1970 ESTIMATE)

	UNITED STATES		SOVIET UNION	
Number of cities	Percent of population	Percent of industrial capacity	Percent of population	Percent of industrial capacity
10	25	33	8	25
50	42	55	20	40
100	48	65	25	50
200	55	75	34	62
400	60	82	40	72
1,000	63	86	47	82

system could have become operational by 1963-64, but—according to subsequent estimates—would have been obsolete by that time. Other ABM concepts were put forward, including one that would permit Polaris-armed missile submarines to fire their weapons in either an offensive or ABM defensive mode. Research and development were undertaken, however, only on the Nike-Zeus and its direct successors, the Nike-X, Sentinel, and Safeguard systems. All had the promise of being extremely expensive if deployed. (See Figures 6-1, 6-2, 6-3, and 6-4.)

Soviet ABM efforts probably were formalized into a program shortly after the Nike-Zeus. Deployment of advanced defense systems, first reported near Leningrad in 1962, caused speculation as to Soviet ABM deployments, but these systems were later evaluated as advanced anti-aircraft installations. In 1964, the Soviets put on display an ABM missile labeled as the Galosh by NATO. Galosh missile launchers and associated radars subsequently were deployed around Moscow. Within three to four years, the system consisted of the large ABM-associated radars and 64 interceptor missiles, with one- or two-megaton warheads and an estimated range of 200 miles.

With this evidence of a potential Soviet ABM deployment, the United States initiated a counterdeployment of weapons to overcome ballistic missile defenses. The basic means to counter an ABM system are to saturate the ABM's radars and associated electronic equipment used to track incoming reentry vehicles, or else to exhaust the ABM interceptor missiles. Other methods, such as a preliminary attack on ABM radars (possibly by bombers), are less certain.

To overcome an ABM system, the number of RVs could be increased initially by increasing the number of offensive land-based or sea-based missiles. More missiles, however, means more launch equipment, more crews, more submarines (for the SLBMs), more real estate (for the ICBMs), and so on. Instead, another technological approach to saturating ABM interceptors was undertaken—i.e., the multiple warhead missile. With multiple warheads, a single missile carries aloft several RVs which are released in flight to come down separately against one or more targets. A simplistic analogy is the single, large bullet compared to buckshot. The development of more accurate controls for rocket motors, computers, miniaturized electronics, and inertial navigation made multiple warheads feasible.

Multiple Warhead Development

The United States began deployment of the first multiple warhead on the Polaris submarine-launched missile. In 1964, the Polaris A-3 became operational. With a range of 2,500 nautical miles, the A-3 missile greatly increased the ocean areas in which Polaris submarines could operate and remain within missile range of Moscow and other inland Soviet targets. The A-3 variant carries a Multiple Reentry Vehicle (MRV) payload. As each Polaris A-3 missile streaks aloft, the warhead separates into three separate RVs, or "bomblets," that can strike a single target. The dispersion of the RVs insures more damage to the target than a single warhead with the same degree of accuracy. Whereas the Polaris A-1 and A-2 warheads were generally described as being about one megaton in explosive force, the A-3 missile's three RVs each have an explosive force of only some 200-KT because of the additional weight and space required for the separation apparatus (the Post-Boost Vehicle, or PBV). Still, although the sum of the three RVs is less than the Polaris A-1 and A-2 payload, the pattern effect of three RVs would result in greater overall destruction to a soft target, such as a city or railroad marshalling complex. The first Polaris submarine armed with the multiple-warhead A-3 missiles, the USS *Daniel Webster*, went to sea in 1964. Subsequently, most of the Navy's 41 ballistic missile submarines were rearmed with the A-3 missile; the others were rearmed with the more-advanced Poseidon (see chart below).

Although the A-3 warhead was intended to increase damage, and was not specifically designed to evade missile defenses, it was less vulnerable to an ABM intercept system. However, development was already underway on Multiple Independently targeted Reentry Vehicle (MIRV) warheads that could send RVs against separate targets. The MIRV rocket boosters carry aloft a "bus" containing the individual RVs. After the boosters burn out and fall away, the bus continues toward enemy territory, releasing the RVs in sequence. After each release, the orientation and velocity of the bus is changed by a preset program to aim the next RV release. Obviously, the area of land, or "footprint," in which the separate RVs can be aimed is limited, and all must fall within the overall range of the missile. Still, MIRV technology means that one missile can attack several, separated targets.

The first US tests of an operational MIRV system began in 1968 with the Minuteman-III, an ICBM with a nominal range of 7,000 nautical miles. Whereas the earlier Minuteman-I and -II missiles carried a single warhead of about one megaton, the warhead of the Minuteman-III has three RVs with a yield estimated at from 170-KT to 200-KT each. Between 1970 and mid-1973, 550 of the earlier Minuteman ICBMs in the SAC arsenal were replaced by Minuteman-III missiles with MIRV warheads.

In 1970, the first submarine firings were conducted with the submarine-launched Poseidon C-3 missile. This MIRV weapon, the successor to the Polaris A-3 missile, has a reported range of some 2,000 nautical miles and can deliver up to 14 RVs, each with a yield of about 50-KT. Fewer RVs can be carried to increase the range to about 2,500 miles. Between 1970 and 1978, the US Navy converted 31 of its Polaris submarines so to enable each to fire 16 of the Poseidon MIRV missiles, generally carrying ten RVs. (The ten oldest Polaris submarines were not suitable for modification to the newer weapon, and carried the A-3 missile until they were retired in 1980-81.)

The Minuteman and Poseidon MIRV programs increased by more than fourfold the number of reentry vehicles of the US strategic offensive forces, easily providing the capability to overcome any foreseeable Soviet ABM system and still destroy at least 400 Soviet cities. When the US multiple-warhead programs were completed in 1978, the inventory of US long-range missiles consisted of:

US STRATEGIC MISSILE WARHEAD CAPABILITY
(1970s)

Pre-MIRV	Post-MIRV
1,000 Minuteman	54 Titan-II
54 Titan-II	450 Minuteman-II
	1,650 Minuteman-III
656 Polaris	160 Polaris A-3
	4,960 Poseidon C-4
1,710	7,274

Defensive Systems

With respect to defensive systems, the US-Soviet agreement resulting from the Strategic Arms Limitation Talks (SALT) in 1972 restricted ABM deployments. Under this agreement, each nation was allowed to build and operate one ABM site in defense of the national capital and another in defense of an ICBM base. Each site was defined according to area, number of missile launchers, and types of radars. This aspect of SALT permitted the Soviet Union to maintain the Galosh ABM already emplaced around Moscow (which also defends some ICBMs in that area), and the United States to continue construction of a Safeguard ABM being installed near Grand Forks, North Dakota, intended to defend 150 Minuteman ICBMs. In SALT, the United States gave up a much-emaciated ABM program that was just put forward in 1967 to provide a full-fledged missile defense against Chinese Communist missiles, and then—in 1969—to defend the Minuteman ICBMs against a Soviet attack. On June 28, 1974, the allowable ABM sites were further reduced. Meeting in Moscow, President Nixon and Party Secretary Brezhnev agreed to retain only the ABM sites at Grand Forks and Moscow, and to give up the option of building a second site. Construction of the US site at Grand Forks had already been halted in 1972. A few years later the Department of Defense announced that the ABM facilities would be converted to peaceful, civilian uses. The Soviet ABM site at Moscow—with 64 intercept missile launchers—survived until about 1980, when approximately half of the launchers were observed being dismantled. This activity indicated the probable installation of a new ABM system to defend the Soviet capital, a move allowed within the context of the expired but still partly observed SALT I agreement.

Another ABM concept that received consideration in the 1960s was the US Navy's proposal for a Sea-based Ballistic Missile Intercept System (SABMIS). This concept provided for deploying anti-missile ships in the North Atlantic and North Pacific where their interceptor missiles could shoot down Soviet- or Chinese-launched ICBMs. The advantages of the forward-deployed ships would include early intercept, before multiple warheads fully separated and hence were easier to kill; moreover, the intercepts would take place over the sea and not the United States or Canada, and the launch of interceptor missiles would not interfere with ICBM launches from the United States as would collocated ABM/ICBM systems. Studies indicated that the SABMIS ships—working either independently or with terminal defenses in the United States—would be both survivable and effective. SABMIS was rejected, however, primarily because of US interservice policies which favored maintaining an Army role in continental air-missile defense; hence, only the (limited) Safeguard ABM program was put forward for consideration by the US government.

While ABM programs have had the major attention in the strategic arms arena, three other aspects of strategic defense are significant: surveillance and warning, anti-aircraft defenses, and civil defense. (Of course, anti-submarine efforts against SLBM submarines are also a form of strategic defense. However, it is difficult to always distinguish ASW against these submarines from efforts against tactical or attack submarines.)

US efforts to provide early warning of a possible Soviet air attack began in earnest in the mid-1950s with the expansion of the Soviet long-range bomber force. The joint US-Canadian North American Air Defense Command (NORAD) was formed in 1958 placing the air defense of both countries under a single commander, an American. At the same time, a number of warning systems were being built. Reaching a peak in the 1960s, this development included a chain of 81 Distant Early Warning (DEW) radar stations strung across Canada, Greenland, and Alaska, continuously airborne EC-121 radar warning aircraft, and Navy radar picket ships at sea, all linked to the elaborate NORAD/CONAD (US Continental Air Defense Command) control centers.

Then, with the advent of ICBMs, the United States initiated the Ballistic Missile Early Warning System (BMEWS) with huge, fixed (phased-array) radar antennas in Great Britain, Greenland, and Alaska. These antennas

Figure 4-10. This is a rare surface firing of a Polaris A-2 missile from the USS *Henry Clay*, one of the U.S. Navy's 41 Polaris submarines. These SLBMs are normally fired while the submarine is fully submerged. (The tall mast is a temporary telemetry antenna installed for the test launch.) The submarine design permitted subsequent carrying of the improved Poseidon and later Trident-I missiles with minimum modifications. (U.S. Navy)

Figure 5-1. Three Soviet and Eastern bloc ships are shown reloading missile support equipment at the Cuban port of Mariel in this photograph taken on November 2, 1962. A short time before, the ships had unloaded missiles, their support equipment, and other weapons in Cuba. This photo was taken by a low-flying U.S. Navy RF-8A Crusader aircraft. (U.S. Navy)

Figure 5-2. Crewmen uncover one of the crates containing fuselages for Il-28 Beagle light bombers aboard the Soviet merchant ship *Kasimov*. The Soviets sent 42 of these aircraft to Cuba in the fall of 1962. Although generally considered "tactical" aircraft, from Cuba they could reach targets in the United States. The *Kasimov* carried 15 of the knocked-down aircraft out of Cuba after the American-Soviet showdown. (U.S. Navy)

Figure 5-3. This heavily retouched photograph shows the relative size of the Soviet SS-9 Scarp intercontinental missile. When the SS-9 entered Soviet service in 1967 it could lift a heavier payload than any other U. S. or Soviet ICBM. One variant could deliver a 25-MT warhead against targets, while others were fitted with multiple warheads. The 288 SS-9 missiles deployed in the late 1960s have been replaced by the improved SS-18 "heavy" ICBM.

Figure 5-4. This series shows a Titan-I missile being raised from a hardened, underground silo in a demonstration at Vandenberg Air Force Base in California. All U.S. and Soviet ICBMs are similarly deployed. The later Titan-II is the only U.S. "heavy" ICBM. Although it was planned that Titan-II would be phased out in the 1970s, 52 of the missiles survive to give the United States a capability of striking "hard" targets such as protected, underground command centers. (U.S. Air Force)

Figure 5-5. Further improvements led to the Minuteman-III. Here two missiles are launched from Vandenberg Air Force Base in a 1979 operational test. Each missile carried aloft three Mk-12A dummy warheads that came down near Kwajalein atoll. U.S. strategic missiles cannot be tested over the United States; thus "operational" missiles must be trucked and flown from their silos to Vandenberg for test or exercise launches. (U.S. Air Force)

Figure 5-6. Since the early 1950s, U.S. aircraft carriers have made a significant—albeit often improperly understood—contribution to U.S. strategic capabilities. During the late 1950s, when this photo was taken of the Forrestal-class carrier *Saratoga*, there were four squadrons of nuclear strike aircraft among the 85 planes embarked in the ship. (U.S. Navy)

Figure 6-1. During the 1950s and 1960s the United States emphasized defenses against Soviet bomber attacks. The IM-99 Bomarc was an Air Force-developed interceptor missile (initially designated as a fighter, XF-99). Either a conventional or a nuclear warhead could be fitted for intercepting enemy aircraft, and several Bomarc squadrons were operational in the United States and Canada until the early 1970s. (U.S. Air Force)

Figure 6-2. A Nike anti-aircraft missile explodes on contact with a radio-controlled B-17 drone during a 1953 test launch of the basic U.S. air defense missile of the 1950s and 1960s. Such shots of the U.S. Army-operated missile were impressive, but the lack of enemy jamming and countermeasures made their true relevance questionable. Nike launch sites were scattered throughout the United States, as well as in several European NATO nations, Taiwan, and Japan. (U.S. Army)

Figure 6-3. Shown here is a battery of Nike anti-aircraft missiles at varying degrees of elevation at Lorton, Virginia (a suburb of Washington, D.C.) in May 1955. These are Nike-Ajax versions of the missile. At the peak of Nike deployments there were over 3,000 launchers in the United States and overseas, all linked to regional and national air defense centers. The American missile network has been dismantled, but the Soviet Union retains a massive anti-bomber missile capability. (U.S. Army)

Figure 6-4. This is an early test model of the Nike-Zeus, the first American effort to develop an anti-ICBM or Anti-Ballistic Missile (ABM) system. In 1958 Zeus was selected over a competitive project named Wizard, with initial operational capability set for 1964. The Zeus was never deployed, but developed into the Safeguard and later American ABM concepts, none of which has been deployed. (U.S. Army)

Figure 6-5. The Tu-28P Fiddler is the largest and heaviest interceptor in Soviet service, with a maximum takeoff weight of 96,000 pounds. This aircraft is a sharp contrast to the longtime image of Soviet fighters being small and light. Used mainly in the anti-bomber role by the National Air Defense Force (PVO-*Strany*), the aircraft is shown here with four AA-5 Ash missiles on wing pylons.

Figure 7-1. The Hawker Siddeley Vulcan flew in the strategic bomber role for the Royal Air Force during the late 1950s and the 1960s. With a high subsonic speed and medium combat radius (up to 2,875 miles), the aircraft could carry the Blue Steel 200-mile stand-off missile, free-fall nuclear bombs, or conventional bombs. The Vulcans remain in RAF service in the tactical support role, with their replacement by lighter aircraft underway in the early 1980s. (Royal Air Force)

Figure 7-2. The Royal Navy developed a carrier-based nuclear strike force employing the Blackburn Buccaneer, shown here flying over HMS *Eagle*. The Buccaneer was an excellent aircraft, capable of Mach 0.9 speeds with night/all-weather capabilities. All British large carriers have been discarded, and the surviving Buccaneers have been given over to the RAF. (Royal Navy)

Figure 7-3. *Le Redoubtable* was the first of a series of French strategic missile submarines. Although no American assistance was given in their development, they outwardly resemble U.S. Polaris submarines, with sail-mounted diving planes and 16 tubes for SLBMs aft of the sail structure. These "boats" are dwarfed by the newer U.S. and Soviet strategic missile submarines. (French Navy)

Figure 7-4. A CSS-4—called Long March 3 by the Chinese—streaks skyward during a test launch. Although the Chinese have a large submarine force, including one diesel-electric Golf submarine provided by the Soviets, no SLBM development has been observed. Rather, ballistic missiles and outdated land-based bombers will be the Chinese nuclear delivery systems through the 1980s. (Chinese Ministry of Defense)

Figure 8-1. A Soviet Delta-I-class strategic missile submarine on the surface. This submarine was the world's largest when she went to sea for the first time in 1973. The subsequent Delta-II had 16 missiles versus 12 in this submarine, while the giant Typhoon-class submarines of the Soviet Navy have 20 tubes for long-range SLBMs.

Figure 8-2. A Tu-22M Backfire-B bomber with variable-sweep wings extended for cruise flight. The Soviets reportedly removed the in-flight refueling probes from these aircraft during the late 1970s SALT negotiations with the United States. However, this aircraft photographed in 1978 had the probe fitted. Note the radar-controlled tail cannon; an air-to-surface missile is nested into the lower fuselage. (Swedish Air Force)

Figure 9-1. The ultimate B-52 design: A B-52H with shortened tail fin and camouflaged paint scheme. During the Vietnam War the B-52D models and some later Stratofortresses were used in a tactical bombing role. They are expected to fly on through the 1980s, during the later years armed with long-range cruise missiles to supplement the shorter-range SRAMs and gravity bombs now carried. (Boeing)

Figure 9-2. Armorers look at SRAMs on a rotary launcher in the weapons bay of a B-52. These missiles are intended to destroy Soviet air defenses, to permit the B-52s to penetrate to their primary targets with gravity bombs. Although relatively old and vulnerable, B-52s still can deliver the largest nuclear weapons in the American arsenal. (U.S. Air Force)

Figure 9-3. A prototype Rockwell International B-1A strategic bomber takes to the air. The four-turbojet, Mach 2+ aircraft was developed as a penetration bomber to strike heavily defended targets with gravity bombs and stand-off missiles. A buy of 240 aircraft was proposed for the late 1970s, but was cancelled by President Carter. Note the resemblance in external appearance to the XB-70. (U.S. Air Force)

Figure 9-4. A variable-geometry (swing-wing) B-1A climbs aloft with an F-111, the tactical strike version of the FB-111A medium-range strategic bomber. Both aircraft sweep back their wings for high-speed flight and extend them (as shown here) for takeoff, cruise flight, and landing. The F-111s were used in the tactical strike role in the Vietnam War. (U.S. Air Force)

Figure 9-5. A closeup of a Minuteman ICBM in a silo launcher prior to a test launch. Note the large pre-launch umbilical cables plugged in at the left and the workman in the silo. Some modern Soviet ICBMs make use of a cold-launch technique that permits the potential for rapid reuse of the launch silo. (U.S. Air Force)

were backed up by other radars that sought to provide early warning of an ICBM attack, hopefully detecting the Soviet missiles during their launch trajectory, thus providing the US National Command Authority (the President and the Secretary of Defense) with a few minutes of warning time.

During the 1960s the early warning systems oriented toward aircraft were reduced considerably, and new radars were installed along the US coasts to provide warning of SLBM launches. In addition, warning satellites have been orbited which can monitor the Soviet Union and detect the heat emitted during an ICBM launch. (These satellites have reportedly detected and broadcast a warning when Soviet oil refineries suddenly flamed off gases.)

The USSR has developed similar land-based radars to give warning of US air or missile attack. While less is known in the public forum about Soviet radars, travellers to the USSR have observed giant, phased-array installations along the long periphery of the nation. While US radars intended to detect Soviet bombers approaching North America have been reduced with the shifting of the Soviet threat to missiles, the Soviet National Air Defense Force (PVO-*Strany*) continues to operate massive bomber defenses which include detection radars, some 10,000 missile launchers, and approximately 2,600 modern fighter-interceptors, all controlled by an extensive command system. (See Figure 6-5.) The radars include some Tu-126 Moss radar aircraft (developed from the turboprop Tu-114 transport) that can extend surveillance and intercept control over waters adjacent to the USSR.

While the PVO-*Strany* has retained a bomber defense capability against Western air attack, the small Soviet bomber force has not evoked significant American interest in air defense. During the 1950s the United States undertook a massive deployment of anti-aircraft missiles and (briefly) anti-aircraft guns coupled with related warning and control systems. At peak strength CONAD had 122 fighter-interceptor squadrons and 280 missile batteries in the early 1960s.

Thereafter US air defense declined steadily until, in 1979, the US Aerospace Defense Command (successor to CONAD) and NORAD essentially became part of the US Air Force's Tactical Air Command. Fighter-interceptor strength in 1981 stood at just over 300 aircraft, while all defensive missiles had been scrapped except for a few in Florida, intended to deter a surprise raid by the Cuban air force. Many of the operational fighter aircraft were from reserve units.

The civil defense situation has been somewhat similar. After a massive civil defense program in the 1950s intended to protect large segments of the American population as well as the National Command Authority, the program dissipated during the 1960s. Today it is difficult to determine who is directing US civil defense. Facilities to protect the population or industry are virtually nonexistent, and the protection of the NCA consists of the White House bomb shelter, an alternative shelter/national command post at nearby Camp Ritchie in the Maryland mountains, and a small number of E-4 aircraft (modified Boeing 747 transports) that can provide escape from the Washington area and airborne command facilities for the NCA.

By contrast, the Soviet Union has maintained a large, high-visibility civil defense program intended to protect the military and political leadership of the country plus a large fraction of the population.[27] Of particular significance are the hardened command centers for most levels of military command down to tactical units; their associated communications facilities also are protected.

For the general Soviet population there are more than 15,000 blast-resistant shelters that can protect some 10 to 20 million persons, depending upon shelter occupancy. This is roughly ten to twenty percent of the population in cities of more than 100,000 people. In some cities there

STRATEGIC DEFENSE FORCE LEVELS
(1982)

	United States	*Soviet Union*
Air/Missile Defense Surveillance Radars	59	7,000
Fighter-Interceptors	309	2,600
SAM Launchers	0	10,000
ABM Launchers	0	32

27. The Department of Defense estimated that there are protective shelters for some 110,000 national leaders: the senior national government officials; some 5,000 party and government officials at the national and republic levels; 63,000 party and government leaders at the kray, oblast, city, and urban rayon level; 2,000 managers of key installations; and about 40,000 members of the civil defense staffs. This is in addition to the military leadership and the major command staffs.

are additional facilities that could protect large numbers of persons in an emergency, especially the massive Moscow subway system. However, food and other life-support provisions in the subway system and some facilities are virtually non-existent. The quality and quantity of such provisions at the 15,000 specified shelters vary. Still, the Soviets have accorded high-level recognition to the civil defense program, which is headed by an Army general with the position of deputy minister of defense, and considerable resourses have been allocated to the program. This may mean that the Soviet leadership *perceives* that civil defense is a strategic weapon, and that perception in itself can become a major factor in Soviet decision-making.

The military and political leadership of the West have tended to downgrade the effectiveness and hence the value of a civil defense program. This may be based on costs, or in part on the feeling that only a massive program with a controlled population could be effective; it may also be felt that allocating resources to more strategic offensive or defensive weapons would be a better investment. It must be recognized, however, that the Soviets have made the investment in civil defense—as well as in strategic offensive and defensive weapons.

Multiple Warheads and First Strike

Virtually any technological development in strategic weapons accomplished by one side can be matched by the other, and so it has been with multiple warhead technology. On the Soviet side, the giant SS-9 Scarp provided a weapon to carry aloft multiple payloads. Testing of the SS-9 with a MRV warhead began in August 1968, and Western estimates soon credited the missile with the ability to carry three reentry vehicles of five megatons each. Thus, each RV was larger than any US ICBM warhead except that of the Titan-II.

Soviet multiple warhead development, even of MRVs that would be limited in coverage or "footprint" and targeting as compared to MIRV warheads, meant that the proposed US missile-defense system could be overcome by saturation. Even discounting other Soviet ICBMs and possibly SLBMs, the Soviets could add RVs to the SS-9 force at much lower costs than the United States could add interceptor missiles to an ABM defense system. With its huge payload, the SS-9 might ultimately be developed to carry as many as 25 RVs per missile.

Traditionally, intercontinental missiles have been viewed primarily for attacking opposing strategic offensive forces in a tactic known as "counterforce." However, the effectiveness of ICBMs carrying a single warhead could be limited against an enemy strategic force of about the same size. ICBMs are susceptible to failures. For an ICBM to function perfectly, hundreds of different parts must work within limited tolerances; although the percentage possibilities of individual failures are small, in the aggregate they significantly reduce the effectiveness of an ICBM force. In the late 1960s, Secretary of Defense Melvin Laird judged Soviet ICBMs to have an effectiveness factor of 80 percent. This meant that—on the average—one missile would launch, travel to its target, come within expected accuracy, and detonate properly eight times in ten firings. Hence, if a thousand Soviet ICBMs were fired against one thousand ICBMs in the United States in a preemptive strike, 800 of the Soviet weapons could be expected to destroy their targets. This would leave the United States with about 200 ICBMs ready to launch (assuming no US missiles were launched until after the Soviet attack). Accepting the same 80 percent effectiveness for US missiles, after absorbing a preemptive attack the US force could still destroy 160 cities in the Soviet Union (200 × 0.8 = 160) if each US missile that survives and functions properly were aimed at a separate Soviet city. This second-strike capability would destroy almost a third of the population and over half the industry of the USSR.

The same arguments given above, but with the roles of aggressor and victim reversed, would also serve to deter the United States from launching a preemptive missile attack against the Soviet ICBM force. Thus, one nation could always deter an enemy first-strike against its ICBM force by maintaining the same number of ICBMs as, or a larger number than, the opponent.

Multiple warhead deployments changed these counterforce equations. With MIRV technology, the Soviets could conceivably arm 500 large ICBMs with three warheads each, with each warhead having a yield of five megatons and a quarter-mile accuracy.[28] Soviet leaders could then plan a preemptive strike which would launch the 500 multiple-warhead

---

28. Measured in terms of Circular Error Probable (CEP), which is the radius of a circle within which half of the RVs are expected to fall. According to official statements, the probability of a Minuteman silo being destroyed by a five-megaton warhead is 50 percent with a missile accuracy of 0.6 miles, 80 percent with an accuracy of 0.4 miles, and 95 percent with an accuracy of 0.25 miles. (Based on 1970 statements.)

ICBMs against the thousand US missile silos. With an 80 percent reliability, some 1,200 RVs could be expected to strike their targets (500 × 3 × 0.8 = 1,200), enough to "pose a serious threat to the survivability" of Minuteman, in the words of Secretary Laird. A surprise first strike of this magnitude could destroy almost all of the US land-based ICBMs; possibly ten or a score of US missiles would survive. The Soviet Union, however, would still retain some 500 missiles with which to threaten US cities, in the event that the United States should retaliate against the counterforce strike (which—because of the fact that the ICBMs are emplaced in the midwestern states—would have killed relatively few Americans).

US authorities have not argued *if* such a situation could occur with MIRV, but rather *when* it could occur. Thus, multiple warheads have been a severely destabilizing influence on strategic weapons development. A leading US defense analyst, Dr. D. A. Paolucci, wrote as early as 1966 that MIRV technology was "fundamentally destabilizing":

> If the Soviets develop this technology, US nonmobile, undefended, land-based ICBMs become obsolete. They are too simple to target by Soviet counterforce. In such an environment, the only utility in non-mobile, land-based systems is a spasmodic retaliatory strike. In a MIRV world, sea-based systems—or mobile land-based systems—appear to be the only alternative available to insure a stable assured destruction capability.[29]

---

29. In a classified staff paper; extracts published on an unclassified basis in Dominic A. Paolucci, "Poseidon and Minuteman: Either, Or; Neither, Nor?" *Naval Institute Proceedings*, August 1968, pp. 46-58. At the time Dr. Paolucci was a captain in the Navy and assigned as Deputy Director, Navy Strategic Offensive and Defensive Systems.

7

The Other Nuclear Powers

US and Soviet development of strategic nuclear weapons was followed—as could have been expected—by British, French, and mainland Chinese efforts.

Great Britain
During World War II, the United States and Great Britain collaborated fully on the development of the atomic bomb. Because Britain was subject to German air attack at the time the decisions were being made, the actual research and development were undertaken in the United States. After the war, the US Congress passed the McMahon Atomic Energy Act, precluding any exchange of information on the design of nuclear weapons between the United States and any other country. This legislation not only showed the American determination to retain a monopoly of nuclear weapons technology as long as possible, but also helped shape initial US attitudes toward nuclear forces developed by its European Allies. At the time, no other Western nation had either fissionable material or the means of manufacturing nuclear weapons.

British scientists—some of whom had worked at US atomic facilities during the war—produced the first British nuclear device, which was exploded on October 3, 1952, in an island group 50 miles northwest of Australia. It was another two years before actual weapons were available.

The British conducted tests of atomic and hydrogen bombs in 1956-57 using the newly delivered Valiant B Mk 1 aircraft. This was a four-jet, swept-wing bomber with a high subsonic speed and a strike radius of just over 2,000 miles. The first Valiant bombers entered service in 1955, and they served for nine years before metal fatigue caused their grounding in 1964 and subsequent disposal.

The Valiant, which was the first of the British V-bombers, was followed by the delta-wing Vulcan, which began entering RAF bomber squadrons in May 1957. (See Figure 7-1.) This was also a four-jet aircraft, slightly larger than the Valiant (200,000 pounds compared to 175,000), but with a transonic speed (630 m.p.h. or Mach 0.95 at 55,000 ft.) and a strike radius of 2,300 miles on high-altitude missions. The initial Vulcan B Mk I, which could deliver a free-fall nuclear weapon, was followed into service in 1962 by the slightly larger and higher-thrust B Mk 2 variant. This aircraft was fitted to carry the Blue Steel air-to-surface missile, credited with a range of 200 nautical miles while delivering a nuclear warhead. The third and last British V-bomber was the Victor, a four-engine, crescent-wing aircraft that entered service in small numbers beginning in 1958. With a performance similar to the Vulcan, the Victor also could carry the Blue Steel missile.

By the early 1960s, the RAF Bomber Command reached a postwar peak strength of some 180 Vulcan and Victor aircraft, with many of the aircraft armed with the Blue Steel missile. However, even the 200-nautical mile stand-off range of Blue Steel was considered insufficient to overcome the increasing capabilities of Soviet air defenses. To extend the stand-off range and hence the survivability of the V-bombers, the British government negotiated to obtain the 1,000-nautical mile, air-launched Skybolt missile under development in the United States. Shortly after the Skybolt test program began in 1962, however, the project was cancelled by Secretary McNamara for technical and economic reasons. This meant the end of the strategic bomber in the RAF.

In late December 1962, President Kennedy offered the British government the technology necessary to develop Polaris-armed, nuclear-propelled submarines. Previous US assistance had resulted in construction of the first British nuclear submarine, HMS *Dreadnought*, which was launched late in 1960. Thus, the decision was made in 1962 that Great Britain would go to an all-missile, seaborne deterrent.

In addition to strategic aircraft, several British tactical aircraft were fitted to carry nuclear weapons, including the highly effective, carrier-based Buccaneer, which has remained in RAF tactical service after Britain's last conventional aircraft carrier was decommissioned in 1979. (See Figure 7-2.) Another RAF nuclear strike aircraft, the TSR-2, was a Mach 2 aircraft which was to have had a combat radius in excess of 1,000 miles; the TSR-2 was cancelled prior to entering service.

Before moving to a sea-based strategic force, the British government did investigate land-based strategic missiles. Early in 1954, Britain began development of an IRBM fired from an underground silo. Named Blue Streak, this would be a second-strike or deterrent weapon, intended to ride out a Soviet attack. Because Soviet strategic weapons were based only 1,200 miles from Britain, however, sufficient accuracy would be available to the Soviets at an early date to destroy the Blue Streak IRBMs even in their hardened, underground silos. Accordingly, in 1960 the Blue Streak program was cancelled for both military and economic reasons. Almost simultaneously the United States was establishing Thor IRBMs in Britain under joint USAF-RAF control. Beginning in 1958, some 60 of these 1,500-nautical mile nuclear weapons were emplaced in Britain. The Thor system was shortlived, however, and the IRBMs were phased out by late 1963.

Britain had to rely on the remaining V-bombers for a strategic offensive force until the Royal Navy's first Polaris submarine was completed late in 1968. That submarine, HMS *Renown*, carries 16 Polaris A-3 missiles provided by the United States, but fitted with British-made MRV warheads. Originally, five submarines were planned (carrying 80 missiles), which would have permitted at least two to be at sea continuously (with 32 missiles). However, the plan for a fifth Polaris submarine was rescinded in February 1965 after the new Labor government took office. The fourth British Polaris submarine was completed in late 1969, and enables the Royal Navy to maintain at least one and periodically two Polaris submarines at sea on deterrent patrol. The nuclear strike responsibilities were formally transferred from the V-bombers to the Polaris submarines on July 1, 1969.

During the 1970s the Polaris provided Britain with an independent deterrent force, although its targeting was part of US-NATO targeting plans. With American development of the MIRV-warhead Poseidon, consideration was given by the British government to refitting the four submarines with that missile. Instead, however, the British developed a Maneuverable Reentry Vehicle (MaRV)-type multiple warhead, designated Chevaline. Originally called Super-Antelope after the proposed American scheme of a Polaris payload that included decoys as well as multiple warheads, the Chevaline carries multiple warheads for attacking a single target, but the reentry vehicles dispensed by the bus or Post-Boost Vehicle (PBV) can maneuver to avoid Soviet defensive missiles, and carry decoys with the same radar reflection characteristics of a real RV.

Even this update would not keep the Polaris submarines at sea indefinitely, and by the late 1970s the question of the next-generation British strategic system was a major issue. Replacement of the four Polaris submarines would be required from the late 1980s onward after some 25 years of service. After considering a number of SLBM options, in mid-1980 the British government decided to replace the Polaris submarines with four or five new undersea craft that would carry the US Trident-I missile. The new submarines would be smaller than their US counterparts and carry only 16 missiles each. The missiles themselves, with a range of some 4,000 nautical miles, would have the US Navy's MIRV capability but with British-made warheads.

The Trident thus would insure the maintenance of a British strategic striking force well into the 21st century.

France

The French government initiated studies of strategic weapons immediately after World War II. With the help of V-2 technology and German scientists, the French developed a missile designated Veronique, generally similar to the V-2 but unsuccessful for a strategic role. The development of atomic weapons followed, and on February 13, 1960, an atomic device was exploded in the Sahara Desert south of Reggan.

Reportedly, the French government approached the United States for assistance in developing missiles to deliver a nuclear warhead. No assistance was forthcoming, and programs were initiated to develop a land-launched missile (SSBS) and a submarine-launched missile (MSBS).[30] As an interim strategic weapon system until the missiles became available, the French relied on the Mirage IV-A jet bomber developed in the 1950s. The Mirage IV-A is a delta-wing aircraft powered by two turbojets that can push the aircraft to a maximum speed of 1,454 m.p.h. (Mach 2.2

---

30. *Sol-Sol Balistique Stratégique* and *Mer-Sol Balistique Stratégique*.

at 40,000 ft.), making it slightly faster than the fastest US strategic bomber, the B-58 Hustler (Mach 2.1). The French aircraft was considerably smaller (73,800 pounds versus 165,000 pounds), however, with about the same 1,200-mile tactical radius. This meant that it, too, required in-flight refueling from tanker aircraft to reach Soviet targets as far as Moscow or beyond.

The original Mirage IV-A flew in June 1959, but extensive redesign delayed introduction of the strategic bomber into combat squadrons until 1964. Thirty-four Mirage bombers remain in strategic squadrons, each aircraft capable of carrying a single, free-fall 70-KT bomb.[31] Some of the Mirages are kept on 15-minute ground alert. Although the United States did not provide assistance in the development of French strategic weapons, 12 American-built KC-135F aircraft were sold to France to permit some of the Mirages to remain on airborne alert during periods of crisis. All but a few of the Mirage bombers are scheduled to be phased out in 1985, with the surviving planes probably being armed with an air-to-surface nuclear missile.

The second-generation French strategic force consists of SSBS missiles. Originally 27 silo-emplaced missiles were planned, but only 18 were actually deployed in the Plateau d'Albion from 1971 onward. Also, it was initially proposed that the SSBS missiles would replace the Mirage bombers, but both systems were retained under a strategic air command established in January 1964 as part of the French strategic force, initially called *force de frappe* and later *force de dissuasion*. (See Figure 7-3.)

The original SSBS was the S-2 with a range of 1,500-nautical miles carrying a 150-KT warhead. In 1978 one nine-missile squadron was taken out of service to be replaced starting in 1980 with the S-3 missile. With a similar range, the S-3 has a 1.2-MT warhead. The other nine SSBS missiles were scheduled for later replacement by the S-3 type.

The third-generation French strategic force consists of nuclear-propelled submarines, each armed with 16 MSBS missiles. The French submarine force is interesting because the MSBS submarine introduced nuclear propulsion to the French Navy, whereas the US, British, and Soviet navies all built torpedo-attack submarines with nuclear propulsion prior to embarking on missile submarine programs. Ironically, the submarine *Gymnote* had been started in 1958 as the first French nuclear submarine,

---

31. The total Mirage IV-A program consisted of 1 prototype, 3 preproduction, and 62 production aircraft.

but the project was cancelled; subsequently, the submarine was completed in 1966 with diesel-electric propulsion to serve as a test platform for the MSBS system.

Five French MSBS submarines, led by *Le Redoutable,* were completed between 1970 and 1980. Similar in many respects to US and British missile submarines, the French craft each carry 16 missiles. The first two units were completed with the M-1 MSBS, with a range of 1,500 nautical miles and a warhead of 500-KT. These missiles were then replaced by the M-2 and, after 1977, the M-20. The M-2 had a range and warhead similar to the M-1, but with several improvements. The M-20, with the same second-stage motor as the land-based S-3, carries the 1.2-MT warhead.

Even before the last French MSBS submarine was completed, the decision had been made to provide a fourth-generation strategic force of improved missile submarines. The 1979 defense budget provided funds to start a sixth missile submarine of the improved *L'Flexible* class. Estimated to be completed in 1985-86, the new submarine will carry the M-4 missile, which would constitute France's first MIRV-warhead weapon. This would be a three-stage weapon, possibly providing a striking range of up to 2,100-nautical miles. The M-4 reportedly will have up to six RVs, each with a 100-KT explosive force.

Current French planning calls for five *L'Flexible*-class submarines to be completed through the early 1990s. This is an extensive strategic weapons program, coupled with modernization of the SSBS force and retention of the Mirage bomber force at least until 1985. Beginning after the British strategic program, the French program has developed at an accelerated rate. In several respects, the French capability is superior to the British strategic force (which now is limited to four SLBM submarines). Because of the lack of US assistance, the French program has cost comparatively more resources than the British effort.

China

The People's Republic of China became the fifth nuclear power when it detonated a nuclear device in the desert area of Sinkiang Province in October 1964. Soviet military assistance to Communist China had begun with the Communist takeover in 1949, and soon extended to a number of armament and technological categories. In 1957, the Soviet Union agreed to provide China with extensive defense technology, technical assistance, and specialized training, including cooperation in atomic matters.

According to Khrushchev, the Soviets had "packed up" a prototype atomic bomb and only at the last minute decided against sending the weapon to China. Khrushchev stated that:

> We kept no secrets from them [the Chinese]. Our nuclear experts cooperated with their engineers and designers who were busy building an atomic bomb. We trained their scientists in our own laboratories.[32]

By 1964, a small but efficient gaseous nuclear diffusion plant was completed at Lanchow;[33] and on October 16, 1964, the first Chinese nuclear device was exploded. Coincidently, this was the same day on which Khrushchev was ousted as head of the Soviet government and Communist Party. (Khrushchev's downfall was caused, in part, by the Sino-Soviet split.)

Along with technical assistance, the Soviets provided the Chinese with weapons that could become "strategic" nuclear delivery systems in the context of a Soviet-Chinese conflict. The initial bomber aircraft in the Chinese Air Force were Soviet-supplied Il-28 Beagle light bombers. These were the same aircraft that Khrushchev had sent to Cuba in 1962. They could carry a single nuclear weapon about 1,200 miles on a one-way flight. Thus, Chinese-based bombers could barely reach the Soviet industrial centers of the Ural mountains, but not the major cities in European Russia. These aircraft obviously posed no threat to the United States.

About 1964, the Chinese assembled a Golf-class, diesel-electric-propelled missile submarine. The submarine was one of a number of Soviet-design undersea craft constructed in Chinese shipyards, initially with Soviet technical assistance and components. The single Golf SLBM submarine appears to have been in limited service from the early 1960s onward. The boat was employed in missile development but was never fully operational. A second SSB-type submarine was reported by Western

---

32. Khrushchev, *Khrushchev Remembers—The Last Testament*, p. 268.
33. Gaseous diffusion is the process whereby natural uranium is gasified to extract the relatively light uranium-235 atoms which are suitable core material for use in fission warheads.

intelligence in 1980, but no details were available when this edition went to press.

By the late 1960s, the Chinese Air Force was credited with also having a few Tu-4 Bull piston bombers (Russian copies of the American B-29). Several of these piston bombers—which could reach targets in European Russia (if unopposed)—may have survived in Chinese service into the 1980s. About 1970, the Chinese aviation industry began producing an indigenous version of the subsonic (Mach .85), jet-propelled Tu-16 Badger bomber, designated B-6 in China. These aircraft were more effective than their predecessors. Production of both the I1-28 Beagle and the Tu-16 Badger bombers has continued, with about 200 of the light bombers and 60 of the medium bombers currently in service. The sale of intercontinental Boeing-707 jet transports to China in the early 1970s and subsequent US-China trade agreements provide the People's Republic of China with the technology for developing advanced bombers. However, the Chinese leadership apparently has decided to concentrate instead on ballistic missiles for the delivery of nuclear warheads.

The nuclear tests conducted during the later 1960s included at least one nuclear weapon carried by a ballistic missile. Deployment of a Medium-Range Ballistic Missile (MRBM) with a range of 700 to 1,000 nautical miles, capable of carrying a warhead of about 20-KT, was predicted for the end of 1968 by Western intelligence. The deployment was delayed, possibly because of technical problems or the Great Proletarian Cultural Revolution.

By the early 1970s the MRBM was in production, based on the design of the Soviet SS-4 Sandal. Western intelligence assigned the designation CSS-1 to the weapon, of which an estimated 50 to 90 have been deployed. Chinese ballistic missile development continued at a rapid pace, with the CSS-2 IRBM and the CSS-3 ICBM becoming operational during the 1970s. The CSS-2 was credited by observers in the West with a range of some 1,350 nautical miles, while the CSS-3 was estimated to be able to deliver a warhead against a target 3,780 nautical miles away. The latter missile could bring Moscow within range of Chinese nuclear weapons. Both the CSS-2 and the CSS-3, like the earlier CSS-1, are liquid fueled, with the newer weapons able to carry a warhead estimated at 3-MT.

However, while about 15 to 20 of the CSS-2 were produced through 1980, only a couple of the CSS-3 missiles are believed to have been manufactured. That missile was abandoned because of development of the CSS-4, at about 200 tons the world's largest ICBM except for the Soviet SS-18. (See Figure 7-4.) However, the limited efficiency of Chinese propellants and engines severely inhibit the capabilities of the CSS-4 missile. The giant weapon can carry a warhead of perhaps 3-MT to a range estimated at 5,400 nautical miles. The ICBM therefore could strike all of the Soviet Union and some portions of the United States.

Until mid-1980, the missile had been flight tested only within China at reduced ranges. CSS-4 boosters were used to launch a series of five heavy, 1,000-pound reconnaissance satellites between 1975 and 1978. Full-range testing was conducted in late May 1980 when two unarmed missiles lifted off from the remote Xinjiang region and traveled to an impact area near the Solomon islands in the South Pacific, monitored by a flotilla of 18 Chinese tracking and support ships. Operational deployment of the CSS-4—called the Long March 3 by the Chinese—is expected by the mid-1980s. The Chinese missiles share with the bomber force the potential for limited strikes against the Soviet Union. Indeed, reportedly six of the 12 nuclear devices exploded by China through 1980 were dropped by Tu-16/B-6 aircraft. Despite efforts aimed at the development of an SLBM, the Chinese appear to have concentrated on land-launched strategic missiles. Future Chinese R&D in the ballistic missile field can be expected to emphasise accuracy, engine efficiency, and possibly multiple warheads.

India

Beyond the five major world powers, observers had long speculated on which nation would be the next to detonate a nuclear device. Candidate nations for this dubious distinction have included Brazil, India, Israel, Japan, the Netherlands, Sweden, West Germany, and Iraq. These nations and several others have been engaged in "peaceful" nuclear research efforts. India's efforts were aided by Canadian technical assistance and uranium.

India exploded a low-yield nuclear device in the Rajasthan Desert area on May 17, 1974. The Indian government promptly labeled the 10- to 15-KT explosion as "peaceful," and disclaimed any military intent. Semantics aside (for no one has yet demonstrated a peaceful use for a nuclear explosion), and despite considerable speculation, the Indian nuclear device does not constitute a strategic nuclear capability. At least for the near future, the actual weapons and effective means of delivery against the principal cities or industrial centers of China and the Soviet Union do not exist. The only strike aircraft in the Indian Air Force are ex-British Canberra light bombers and Soviet-type fighter-bombers.

The Third World

India used uranium that was not considered to be weapons-grade material in its 1974 atomic device. That fact reinforced the beliefs of those who had predicted that any Third World state with a reactor and the proper technology could produce uranium or even plutonium suitable for nuclear weapons.

The response in neighboring Pakistan to the Indian detonation was immediate concern. Zulfikar Ali Bhutto, head of the Pakistani government, had declared that "if India builds the bomb, we will eat leaves and grass, even go hungry, but we will have to get one of our own." When Pakistan's first nuclear power plant was completed in 1972, with Canadian assistance, Bhutto pledged that Pakistan would use nuclear energy only for peaceful purposes. After the Indian test, however, a Pakistani official declared that the government was "reexamining its nuclear priorities." Subsequently, there has been increased suspicion that nuclear research in Pakistan has been stepped up, with Qaddafi of oil-rich Libya providing the funds for both research and nuclear intelligence collection, including industrial espionage.

Also in the wake of India's atomic blast, the Shah of Iran reportedly told the French magazine *Les Informations* that Iran was planning to develop nuclear weapons. A few days later, however, the Iranian Embassy in Paris published a statement, coinciding with the Shah's arrival in the French capital, that denied the earlier statement. All possibility for the foreseeable future of Iranian development of nuclear weapons probably ended with the ouster of the Shah, the cutoff of US technical assistance, and the Islamic revolution that tore the country asunder in 1979-81.

The Iraqi government entered the nuclear field in 1959 through an agreement with the Soviet Union for the construction of a small reactor outside of Baghdad. More significantly, in the 1970s, as Saddam Hussein, Iraq's ambitious leader, sought to make his country the most powerful in the the Arab world, he turned to France and Italy for advanced nuclear technology. This program included a powerful research reactor and a plutonium-separation plant capable of making weapons-grade fuel.

Meanwhile, Iraq attacked its long-time antagonist Iran in mid-1980, taking advantage of the cutoff of US military supplies to Iran and the internal tumult in the country. During the campaign, which included air strikes by both sides, there was an air strike against Iraq's nuclear research facility near Baghdad. While the strike appeared to be made by Iranian planes, there were immediate rumors that the raid, on September 30, 1980, was in fact made by Israeli F-4 Phantoms. A short time after the raid a group of French engineers who worked in the Iraqi nuclear program declared that the reactor had been secretly modified to produce plutonium outside of international controls.

While there was no direct evidence of Soviet assistance to Iraq in the development of nuclear weapons, the Russians had provided the potential delivery means in the Scud-B ballistic missiles, with a range of some 150 miles, and Tu-22 Blinder aircraft which could carry free-fall weapons, plus various tactical fighter-attack aircraft, which could reach targets in either Iran or Israel.

Israeli intelligence was alert to the massive expansion of Iraqi nuclear efforts. Israeli efforts failed to gain enhanced international safeguards against the Iraqi production of weapons-grade material. As covert actions by Israeli intelligence failed to appreciably slow the Iraqi program, on June 7, 1981, Israeli-piloted F-16 fighter-bombers struck the French-built Osirak reactor some ten miles from Baghdad. Given the code name Babylon, the raid consisted of eight F-16s, with an escort of six F-15 fighters (all American-built), successfully flying through some 650 miles of hostile air space over Jordan, Saudi Arabia, and Iraq to deliver their 2,000-pound bombs on the nuclear facility. Reportedly, all 16 bombs struck the target as each plane made a single pass. The Israelis suffered no losses in the precision strike. Operation Babylon, carried out on a Sunday to avoid casualties among some 150 French and 50 Italian technicians working at the facility, was considered a military success, although there was severe criticism of the Israeli action in the West as well as in the Arab world.

Israel itself has long been rumored to have developed nuclear weapons. The Israeli government periodically has denied that it possesses nuclear weapons; but on December 1, 1974, President Ephraim Katzir stated that Israel "has the potential" to make an atomic weapon, "and if we need it, we will do it." He did not state how long it would take Israel to produce a weapon, or under what circumstances it would be developed. The French-built research reactor at Dimona in Israel can produce plutonium, and some observers have speculated that enough material had been produced through 1975 for the manufacture of five to ten nuclear weapons.

The most definite information that the Israelis now possess nuclear weapons came in August 1975, when the Boston *Globe* reported that Israel had an arsenal of ten nuclear weapons. The writer was William Beecher, former defense correspondent for *The New York Times,* who had recently returned from a three-week trip to Israel and Egypt. Mr. Beecher's report had special significance: he had served as Deputy Assistant Secretary of Defense for Public Affairs in the Pentagon from 1973 to May 1975. Little more was said on the subject of an Israeli atomic bomb until September 22, 1979, when an atmospheric explosion over a remote part of the South Atlantic was detected by a US Vela nuclear-test detection satellite. Subsequently, related radioactive fallout was detected in New Zealand two months later.

On November 13, 1979, a US official reportedly said that "Radioactive fallout was the key missing element in what we thought originally was a clandestine nuclear test." The fallout in New Zealand could well have been that "missing element." Other American officials voiced the opinion that despite the fallout, the "flash" detected by the Vela satellite was from natural causes. However, in July 1980, the US Defense Intelligence Agency finished its study of the incident and concluded that the flash and other effects were probably caused by a clandestine nuclear explosion.

South Africa denied being the source of "whatever" occurred. However, the close relationship between Israel and South Africa, the large-scale purchase of Israel military equipment by Pretoria, and other factors increase the likelihood that it was an Israeli nuclear device tested in collaboration with the South African government.

One US newspaper has stated that India "let the nuclear genie out of the bottle." In some respects, nuclear weapons are only "bigger bangs" than conventional weapons; the World War II destruction of Hamburg, Dresden, and Tokyo with conventional weapons tends to support this thesis.[34] Nuclear weapons, however, do provide the opportunity for a single attacking bomber or missile to "leak" through a nation's defenses and, with one weapon, destroy an entire city. On the other hand, at the superpower level, strategic weapons and RVs are counted in the thousands.

---

34. Atomic bombs killed an estimated 71,000 persons at Hiroshima and 40,000 at Nagasaki. Conventional bombing attacks killed 83,000 in Tokyo (March 9-10, 1945), 50,000 in Hamburg (July 24-August 3, 1944), and 130,000 in Dresden (February 13-14, 1945). Only rough estimates are available for the two German cities.

8

Today and Tomorrow: The Soviet Union

The Soviet Union completed deployment of its second-generation ICBMs in the early 1970s, with just over 1,600 missiles or more than half-again as many land-based ICBMs as the United States. These were mainly SS-11 "medium" weapons, with a range of some 7,500 nautical miles, carrying a 1- or 2-MT warhead. From 1973 onward some of the deployed SS-11 missiles carried a three-MRV warhead; the three RVs could be shotgunned down onto the same target, with each RV being rated at 100- to 300-KT, according to Western sources. The remaining Soviet ICBMs consisted of 60 of the smaller SS-13, the first Soviet solid-propellant ICBM, which carried a single 1-MT warhead; almost 300 of the giant SS-9 missiles—classified as "very heavy" missiles by US intelligence—with a single 25-MT warhead or three smaller, perhaps 5-MT, MRV warheads; plus a number of older ICBMs. This force was impressive, for although accuracy and reliability are believed to have been significantly less than those of comparative American ICBMs, the number of missiles and their throw weight were awesome.

ICBMs deployed by the Soviet Strategic Rocket Forces had increased by more than 200 missiles per year between 1967 and 1971. (US intercontinental missile deployments had halted at 1,054 in 1967.) The rate of Soviet ICBM deployments slowed in the early 1970s, which gave rise to speculation that the Soviets were about to reach their force level goal.

The number 1,618 was, in fact, agreed to as the upper limit for Soviet ICBMs in the SALT I Agreements.

The first Soviet ICBM to display a multiple warhead was the large SS-9 Scarp. By 1970, there was considerable evidence that the Soviets had successfully tested the Mod 4 version of the SS-9 with a warhead that could carry three five-megaton reentry vehicles in a carefully spaced pattern. Even though the nominal 25-MT payload of the SS-9 is reduced to a total of 15-MT in the multiple warhead version to provide for the separation apparatus, the SS-9 Mod 4 still carried more megatonnage than the largest US strategic missile (the Titan). The three-RV configuration of the SS-9 Mod 4 immediately gave rise to speculation that the weapon was intended specifically for first-strike attacks against the Minuteman ICBM silos, which are arranged in patterns at an average of five miles separation. Later statements by US officials indicated that the MRV-version of the SS-9 probably lacked the accuracy for attacking Minuteman silos and had not been deployed in sufficient numbers to be effective against the US intercontinental missiles.

The Third Generation

Even as the Soviets were attaining this massive deployment of ICBMs, there was evidence that an intensive development program was underway for a new generation of ICBMs. US Secretary of Defense James Schlesinger revealed the extent of the Soviet developments early in 1974 when he told the Congress, "One of the most important developments in the strategic threat during the past year has been the Soviet Union's demonstration of a MIRV technology. While this development had been anticipated for many years, the scope of the Soviet program as it has now emerged is far more comprehensive than estimated even a year ago."

Schlesinger then went on to review the magnitude of the Soviet effort. Four new ICBMs were in development—the SS-16, -17, -18, and -19. All have Post-Boost Vehicles (PBV)—a bus-type dispensing system—for multiple warheads, and all give indications of improved accuracy over their predecessors. However, their other characteristics differ significantly, indicating the breadth and scope of the Soviet ICBM effort, which Schlesinger labeled as "unprecedented."

The two medium missiles (the -17 and -19), are liquid fueled, but with a throw weight three to five times that of their predecessor, the SS-11. The heavy SS-18, which replaces the SS-9, also carries a single, large warhead of perhaps 25-MT. The Mod 2 variant of the SS-18 carries 8 or 10 smaller MIRV warheads. Two of the missiles (the -17 and -18) are "cold launch" weapons, meaning that gas generators "pop" them out of the underground silo, after which their boosters ignite. This technique permits a larger volume missile to be placed in a silo of a given diameter, and inflicts minimal damage to the silo, presenting the possibility of reloading the silo and launching another missile in a relatively short interval.

The enigma of the new generation missiles was the SS-16, the only "light" missile in the group. The weapon was tested with only one RV; however, it carried the PBV or bus normally associated with multiple warheads, indicating that there would be a later version with MIRVs, or—more likely, given the fact that the SS-16 was a light ICBM—it would be a highly accurate weapon. There were also early indications that the SS-16 would be a land-mobile missile, transported on a land vehicle that could change position periodically to make U.S. pre-targeting for a surprise attack difficult.

However, the SS-16 was not deployed, at least not as an ICBM. The US government declared to the Soviets that it would consider the deployment of a land mobile ICBM inconsistent with the terms of the interim SALT agreement. The SS-16 was flight tested only once between 1975-80 as an ICBM, and that was unsuccessful. Without its third-stage booster, the missile's range drops from an estimated 4,200 nautical miles to about 3,000, qualifying it as an IRBM. In that configuration—designated SS-20—it has been extensively deployed in the Soviet Union as a theater weapon. It has subsequently been fitted with a MIRV warhead estimated to carry three 150-KT reentry vehicles, making the missile an effective theater weapon for use against European NATO or China.

While no SS-16 missiles were emplaced, some analysts believe that the SS-20s could be fitted with a third-stage booster in a relatively short time, thus converting them to ICBMs. By July 1981, some 250 of the SS-20s were deployed (175 in European Russia and the remainder presumed in Siberia, where they are targeted against China). The US intelligence community estimated that some 350 to 450 of these three-warhead missiles would be emplaced by the mid-1980s.

The US intelligence community placed total Soviet ICBM strength in 1981 at 1,398 missiles, a decline of some 200 from the peak of a few years earlier. The modernization of Soviet ICBMs was continuing, at the rate of about 125 improved missiles per year. The older weapons (SS-11 and earlier) were already gone or being dismantled as new weapons were being inserted in their silos.

Beyond even the four ICBMs and their several variants that were completed in the 1970s, there were indications that at least four new ICBMs—albeit some which may possibly be further enhancements of previous weapons—were in development for possible deployment in the late 1980s.

Submarine-Launched Missiles

The massive Soviet ICBM program that began about 1967 was accompanied by a similar trend in SLBM deployments. The Golf and Hotel SLBM programs of 1958-62 had provided the Soviet Navy with 93 missiles in 23 diesel and eight nuclear-propelled submarines. The relatively short range of these weapons (initially 300 nautical miles and later 700 nautical miles), the requirement for surface launch with the earlier missiles, the operational mode of these submarines, and the anti-submarine forces of the US Navy made these submarines a minimal strategic threat to the United States.

The first "modern" Soviet SLBM submarine of the Yankee class went to sea in 1968. When the Yankee program ended in 1974, there were 34 of these submarines operational, carrying a total of 544 SS-N-6 missiles with a range of 1,300 nautical miles. Subsequently, tests were conducted with a 1,600 nautical mile, MRV-configured SS-N-6, "Mod 3," apparently a weapon similar to the Polaris A-3 that releases three reentry vehicles onto a single target. In addition, the SS-N-13 ballistic missile, an *anti-ship* weapon with some form of terminal guidance and compatible with the Yankee missile tubes, was also developed, although testing halted in late 1973 and there has been no deployment.

By mid-1975, in addition to the 34 Yankee-class submarines, the Soviet Navy was reported to have at sea almost 15 of the follow-on SLBM submarines of the Delta class. (See Figure 8-1.) This force surpassed the 656 missiles of the US Polaris-Poseidon force. The Delta-I submarine—at about 9,000 tons submerged displacement, with an overall length of 460 feet—was the largest undersea craft constructed to that time. In its original configuration, the Delta has 12 SS-N-8 missiles with a range of 4,200 nautical miles. This means that without leaving Soviet territorial waters, Delta-class missile submarines can target most of the major cities of the United States.

The original Delta-Is were soon replaced on the construction ways at the Severodvinsk shipyard by improved SLBM submarines, first the still-larger Delta-II with 16 tubes for the SS-N-8, and then the Typhoon, a submarine estimated at 25,000(!) tons submerged displacement, with 20 missile tubes. Even before the first Typhoon was completed in early 1981, the Soviets had attained their SALT I limitation of 62 modern missile submarines. Although the provisions of the treaty were technically no longer in force, the Soviets seemed to wish to observe them with respect to missile submarines and to maintain a level of 62-63 submarines. The oldest Yankee-class submarines were withdrawn from service; they apparently have had their missile sections removed and, after modification, are returning to the fleet as torpedo-attack submarines. (By early 1981 the US Navy had about 110 nuclear submarines in commission of all types compared to 170 in the Soviet Navy.)

Still, with 62-63 missile submarines the Soviets can put to sea some 950 modern missiles. These figures are in addition to several older Golf and Hotel class submarines which appear relegated to the theater strike role; six of the Golf submarines are in the Baltic, and the remainder of the submarines in these classes are in the Northern and Pacific fleets.

Whereas the initial Yankee-Delta missiles were single-warhead weapons, in 1974 the SS-N-6 Mod 3 went to sea in a Yankee-class submarine. With a range of 1,600 nautical miles, the Mod 3 has two or three MRV warheads. This was followed by the SS-N-16, which has provided Yankee submarines with a three-MIRV warhead, but still at the relatively short range of some 1,600 nautical miles. A single Yankee has been fitted with the SS-NX-17 missiles, the only solid-propellant SLBM to go to sea. Although this missile has a PBV, it carries only one warhead, again indicating an effort to improve accuracy.

Much more impressive have been the missiles for the Delta-class submarines. The liquid-fueled SS-N-8 with a range of some 4,200 nautical miles was first deployed in 1973. This range meant that a submarine in the coastal waters of the Barents Sea or the almost-enclosed Sea of Okhotsk could target virtually all of the United States with SLBMs. Operating in those coastal waters, the Soviet submarines would be less vulnerable to American anti-submarine activities, especially since they could be protected by land-based aircraft, coastal craft, and even defensive minefields.

The original SS-N-8 missile, with one warhead, was followed in the Delta tubes by the SS-N-18; the Mod 1 version has three MIRVs and the Mod 2 has seven. At the same time Soviet SLBM ranges and accuracy have been improving, their warheads have remained relatively large— larger than their American contemporaries. Most published articles credit the single-warhead Soviet SLBMs with 1- or 2-MT warheads, while the three-MIRV SS-N-18 is believed to have that yield in *each* RV. If the SS-N-18 has an aggregate of even a 3-MT yield, then the missile has more than five times the yield of the contemporary US Poseidon (with 14 warheads), or 4½ times that of the Trident-I (with 8 warheads).

Still another Soviet submarine was observed by Western intelligence in the late 1970s while under construction at the Severodvinsk yard in the Arctic. Labeled ''Typhoon'' by the Soviets, the first of these underwater giants was launched in 1980. With a submerged displacement of some 25,000 tons, the Typhoon represents the largest submarine ever built, about half-again as large as the US Trident submarines. The Typhoon has a radical design, with 20 missile tubes for a new weapon, designated SS-N-20 in the West, fitted forward of the sail structure. While the reasons for the size and radical design of the Typhoon were not publicly known when this monograph went to press, the undersea giant was evidence of the continued and innovative Soviet submarine programs.

Also, the Soviet Navy operates its strategic submarines with different procedures than the US Navy. For example, the Soviet Navy does not ''double-crew'' SLBM submarines in the manner of the US Navy, which alternates crews in order to keep some 50 percent or more of the missile force at sea continuously. Also, Soviet SLBM submarines appear to be faster than the US undersea craft, while their machinery generates more noise. This may indicate Soviet plans to destroy the US acoustic surveillance systems at the outbreak of conflict, or to operate the submarines in areas where they can be defended from US counterforces using acoustic detection.

The overall Soviet SLBM program has enjoyed a high priority in Soviet planning. During the period 1968-80, inclusive, an average of five SLBM submarines per year were built, with 12 Yankees being produced in the peak year. American Polaris production from 1960 to 1967, a shorter period, averaged six submarines. The Soviet production of modern missile submarines has been continuous, however, with the USSR currently producing seven to ten nuclear submarines per year of all types, some of which are missile craft.[35]

Land-Based Bombers

Perhaps the most difficult aspect of Soviet strategic weapons development to measure has been *Aviatsiya Dalnovo Deistviya*, or Long-Range Aviation (LRA). In January 1981, the LRA was estimated to operate:[36]

110	Tu-20 Bear long-range bombers
49	Mya-4 Bison long-range bombers
320	Tu-16 Badger medium bombers
140	Tu-22 Blinder medium bombers
70	Tu-22M Backfire medium bombers

In addition, the Soviet naval arm—*Morskaya Aviatsiya*—flies some 70 Backfires, about 300 Badgers, plus a few Blinders in the anti-ship strike role.

Some 75 of the LRA Bears as well as most of the Badgers and Backfires of both services can carry stand-off missiles. Those of the LRA are intended to strike land targets, while the naval weapons are for use against hostile surface ships. The remaining LRA long-range bombers, half of the force, carry only gravity bombs. Counting the Backfire as well as the Bear and Bison bombers of LRA, the Soviets have relatively few aircraft that could reach the United States. The shorter-range LRA Badgers and Blinders are obviously theater weapons, intended in wartime for strikes against NATO Europe and China. The Backfire's role, however, has been questioned.

The Backfire entered service in 1974. (See Figure 8-2.) It is a twin-engine, high-speed (Mach 1.8) aircraft with variable-sweep wings—i.e., the wings extend for landing and takeoff as well as for cruise flight, but retract inward for high-speed flight. It can carry bombs internally, or two air-to-surface missiles under its wings. The naval version has been seen with the AS-4 missile, credited with a range of 250 nautical miles.

---

35. Total current Soviet nuclear submarine construction capacity is estimated at 15 to 20 units per year. The current capability of US shipyards is five attack submarines and $1\frac{1}{2}$ Trident missile submarines per year.

36. LRA also operates the Mya-4 Bison and Tu-16 Badger aircraft in the tanker role, and the Tu-20 Bear and Tu-16 Badger aircraft in the reconnaissance role.

Concern has been voiced that the Backfire is in fact a strategic bomber, intended for striking the United States. Estimates of the aircraft's range vary, but a combat radius of almost 3,000 miles is generally accepted.[37] Although it is capable of inflight refueling, which would permit intercontinental strikes, the Backfire seems to be a theater strike aircraft in both LRA and naval service. Had the Backfire been intended as an intercontinental bomber, to replace the obsolete Bear and Bison bombers, then it would have been reasonable to expect that most if not all of the first hundred or so Backfires would be assigned to LRA. Instead, one-half of the aircraft produced—a total of about 150 by mid-1981—were sent to Navy anti-ship strike regiments.

Since 1974 the Soviets have alluded to the development of an improved variable-sweep bomber aircraft. However, no definite word of this aircraft has been announced by Soviet or US officials. In view of the decline of LRA as a strategic bomber force during the past two decades, it appears unlikely that the newer aircraft would be intended for strikes against the United States, should it enter service in the mid-1980s or later.

Other Weapons

In addition to the use of Soviet ICBMs and SLBMs and possibly manned bombers as strategic weapons, some US observers have predicted that the Soviet Union could employ other weapons in a strategic attack. These include the Fractional Orbital Bombardment System (FOBS), which the Soviets have flight-tested (employing the SS-9 missile to carry a payload aloft into a partial orbit), and the Multiple Orbital Bombardment System (MOBS), which, in the view of some experts in the field, would be an easy extension of the FOBS concept. With MOBS, the nuclear weapons are placed in full orbit prior to being de-orbited in a nuclear strike. The last FOBS test was in 1971. There is also the continuing question of the strategic role of cruise missile submarines armed with the long-range SS-N-3 Shaddock missile and the improved SS-N-12 later provided to some Echo and Juliett submarines. These weapons present a different and, in some circumstances, more difficult threat to detect than Soviet SLBMs.

Still another factor that should be considered in the Soviet strategic

---

37. This is for a hi-lo-hi mission, including some 400-500 miles at low altitude and about half of that distance at supersonic speeds.

arsenal are the estimated 400 SS-5 Skean IRBM (2,300 mile/1-megaton) and SS-4 Sandal MRBM (1,200 mile/1-megaton), and the 180 SS-20 IRBM (3,000 mile/MIRV) weapons. Although these missiles could not reach the United States, and some are presumed to be aimed against mainland China, they do provide the Soviet Strategic Rocket Forces with a capability for striking forward-based US weapons and bases in Europe, as well as British and French strategic installations. (At the same time, some US strategic weapons are targeted against Warsaw Pact military activities and mainland China, and thus are not targeted against the Soviet Union.)

The difficulty in estimating Soviet capabilities is caused in large part by the asymmetries between US and Soviet strategic weapon systems. In the early 1980s, the United States has advantages with respect to strategic weapons in (1) MIRVs and reentry vehicle technology, (2) guidance technology, and (3) nuclear weapons technology—i.e., smaller weapons with a better yield-to-weight ratio. At the same time, the Soviets have advantages in (1) numbers of launchers, (2) missile payloads, and (3) ongoing missile development and deployment programs. Over the past few years there has been a significant increase in the quality of Soviet weapons. In addition to these differences, there are many unanswered questions concerning Soviet strategic *defensive* capabilities, both ballistic missile defense and ASW. The Soviets have put considerable efforts into these defensive programs and the West has not been able to identify all of the results. These defensive concepts must also be considered in context with the massive Soviet civil defense program.

It is apparent that the Soviet leadership—which has always been impressed by sheer numbers—also perceives value in increasing the capabilities of strategic weapons, as evidenced by weapon deployments, observed research and development, and pronouncements of capabilities and intentions. This situation, coupled with the delays in American strategic weapons development and deployment, could easily lead to Soviet strategic "superiority" in the 1980s: that is, the ability—in the perception of the *Soviet* leadership—to fight and conclude a nuclear war on terms favorable to the Soviet Union. Such "superiority" would include the perceived possibility of conducting a pre-emptive strike against some or all of the US strategic forces, resulting in US capitulation or inability to effectively retaliate.

9

Today and Tomorrow: United States

Current US strategic offensive thinking is based on the TRIAD concept of three separate and distinct types of weapons, each of which is credited with being able to inflict "unacceptable" damage on the Soviet Union (or any other nation) after the United States suffers a surprise nuclear attack. The term TRIAD was conceived in the late 1960s, after the fact, to describe the existence of the land-based strategic bomber and ICBM forces, and the sea-based SLBM submarine force. Thus, TRIAD did not come about through rational planning, but through the development of separate strategic weapon programs. Furthermore, TRIAD does not continue to exist because of rational justification for three strategic forces. Rather, the concept itself became the rationale for the deployment and maintenance of strategic forces, as each attempt of the past two decades to reduce a specific "leg" of the TRIAD or shift emphasis from one "leg" to another has been met with resistance on the basis that the TRIAD was established and correct—in a word, "holy."

The basis for the current US strategic offensive weapons was the Kennedy-Johnson-McNamara programs of the 1960s. Although Secretary of Defense Harold Brown sought to develop a new TRIAD composition, the failure of President Carter to gain reelection aborted his efforts. Instead, in 1981, Secretary of Defense Caspar Weinberger put forward the

"Reagan Strategic Program," which provided for modernization of or improvements in the US strategic bomber, ICBM, and SLBM forces, plus improvements in the strategic communications and control systems.

Land-Based Bombers

The oldest "leg" of the TRIAD is the land-based strategic bomber force, currently consisting of 347 B-52s and 65 FB-111s flown by the Strategic Air Command, supported by a tanker force of 615 KC-135s and several of the new KC-10 aircraft. The SAC bombers are among the oldest U.S. combat aircraft flying: 79 of the B-52D type delivered in 1956-57, 172 of the B-52G type of 1958-61, and 96 of the B-52H type of 1961-62. (See Figure 9-1.) Thus, the "youngest" SAC bomber is some two decades old. The comment is sometimes heard that many SAC crewmen are younger than the aircraft they fly.

While all B-52s were built for high-altitude attacks with gravity nuclear bombs, they have been extensively modified for low-level flight and attack tactics to help them evade Soviet radar detection and interception. Modifications intended to help them penetrate Soviet defenses and accurately deliver nuclear weapons include providing the B-52G/H models with electro-optical viewing devices, infra-red scanners, a variety of warning devices to detect hostile radars, as well as jammers and other "offensive" electronics.

For attacking Soviet targets, the B-52G/H aircraft carry Mk 28 thermonuclear weapons—the largest "warheads" in the US strategic arsenal—plus Short-Range Attack Missiles (SRAMs). The SRAM is a replacement for the Hound Dog missile. It is rocket powered, carries a small nuclear warhead, and has a range of about 100 miles when released from high altitudes and 35 miles when dropped at low altitudes. The SRAM is intended to knock out enemy anti-aircraft defenses and to attack certain targets that have intensive terminal defenses. It is not, however, a stand-off weapon for attacking the principal B-52 targets—i.e., major Soviet cities with their associated military activities. Rather, the Mk 28 gravity bomb is intended for that task.

The B-52G/H aircraft each carry 12 SRAM vehicles on underwing pylons plus another eight SRAMS on a rotary launcher in the rear weapons bay, with the Mk 28 bombs in the forward bay. The B-52D aircraft, which are not intended to strike heavily defended targets, have no SRAM capability, but carry four thermonuclear bombs.

The smaller FB-111 lacks the range and some of the sophisticated penetration capabilities of the B-52. Still, with multiple in-flight refuelings these aircraft can strike targets in the Soviet homeland, and with its wings swept back the FB-111A can reach Mach 2.5 dash speeds. Four SRAMs are carried on wing pylons, plus two more SRAMs or two nuclear weapons in the FB-111's internal weapons bay. (See Figure 9-2.)

Estimates of the effectiveness of these B-52s and FB-111s against Soviet air defenses vary considerably. As noted earlier, the USSR has expended considerable resources in developing an intensive air defense capability. During ten days in December 1972 over North Vietnam SAC lost 15 B-52s to North Vietnamese-fired SAMs despite extensive support from Air Force, Navy, and Marine electronic warfare and tactical strike aircraft. (Between 50 and 70 SAMs were fired for each B-52 downed.)

In discussing the differences between the situation of a strategic attack and a "limited war," former Secretary of Defense Schlesinger observed:

> We must be careful not to draw a false analogy from the Hanoi and Suez Canal air defense experiences. In both those cases, the air defenses were heavily concentrated in a very limited area; moreover, only conventional weapons were employed by the attacking aircraft. In the case of the Soviet Union, the number of places which have to be defended is very large and, consequently, the air defenses are spread over a vast area. Our bombers, in striking back at the Soviet Union, would be penetrating at very low altitudes to avoid the high and medium altitude SAMs and would be using SRAMs to attack the low altitude SAM batteries. Moreover, our bombers would be employing nuclear weapons, only one of which need penetrate to destroy the target and probably much of its air defenses.

SAC bombers striking targets in the Soviet Union would encounter, however, a more sophisticated air defense environment than in North Vietnam. Also significant is the fact that bomber approach routes from the United States are largely predetermined and limited, with some taking aircraft over several hundred miles of Soviet territory before reaching their primary targets. In addition, the Soviet SLBM and cruise missile submarine force comes into the bomber equation because of their ability to strike bomber bases in the United States with a warning time of only 15 minutes or possibly less. Finally, in order to reach the USSR the bombers are dependent upon in-flight refueling by the KC-135 or the new

KC-10 tankers, presenting another set of vulnerability factors in the bomber equation.

Three considerations are generally put forward to support the continued role for strategic bombers. Proponents note that bombers, once launched toward a Soviet target, are "recallable." While the aircraft is in flight the order to attack can be sent and—if necessary—cancelled by the National Command Authority. However, a B-52 would pass into the Soviet air defense zone perhaps two hundred miles from the Soviet arctic coast— still several hundred miles from Moscow, for example. Thus, for an hour or more the B-52 would be over Soviet-controlled territory and certainly not "recallable." In contrast, an ICBM launched from the United States to Moscow would have a flight time of less than 30 minutes, and a Poseidon or Trident SLBM about one-half that time. Thus, while a B-52 is recallable, an ICBM—with assured, overland communications—could also be recalled, and it is possible that an SLBM could be aborted long after the Soviets would have taken action against the incoming B-52s.

The other arguments in favor of the B-52 are that the weapons deployed to shoot down bombers are not useful against ICBMs or SLBMs, causing the Soviets to diversify their defenses, and the B-52s delivering Mk-28 bombs provide the only megaton warheads in the US arsenal other than the aged 9-MT warheads of the Titan-II missiles.

The B-1 Bomber

The B-52 force was estimated when built to have a peacetime service life of some 20 years, meaning that a replacement manned bomber force would be required in the early 1980s. After Secretary McNamara cancelled the B-70 high-altitude bomber and in 1965 directed procurement of the FB-111A for the strategic role, it appeared likely that there would not be another "heavy" bomber built for the United States. However, in March 1969, Secretary of Defense Melvin Laird, under the newly installed Nixon Administration, announced that the FB-111A program would be cut from the McNamara-planned 210 aircraft to about 60, and that funds were being added to the Defense budget for a new, long-range bomber, the Advanced Manned Strategic Aircraft (AMSA). In jargon-oriented Washington, AMSA was the Air Force euphemism for a long-range bomber to succeed the B-52.

Subsequently redesignated B-1,[38] the aircraft was intended as a low-altitude penetration bomber which would streak over heavily defended targets at high-subsonic speed, launching SRAMs *and* gravity thermonuclear bombs. (See Figures 9-3 and 9-4.) Powered by four turbofan engines, the B-1 would weigh 395,000 pounds compared to 480,000 pounds for the B-52G/H and 100,000 pounds for the FB-111A. Although at high altitudes the B-1 was to have a Mach 1.6 to 2 speed, for low-level attacks it would slow to about 600 m.p.h. The unrefueled combat radius with 24 SRAMs or 24 gravity bombs carried internally would be some 3,000 miles, meaning that the B-1 would require in-flight refueling to reach targets in the Soviet Union from American bases.

The Air Force proposed a production run of 240 B-1s to replace the B-52 force. However, the supersonic speed and advanced electronic equipment of the B-1, coupled with rampant inflation, led to an extremely expensive aircraft. The first flight of the B-1A prototype aircraft occurred in December 1974, with a production decision planned for 1976.

The Department of Defense approved production of the B-1 on December 2, 1976, but the following month Jimmy Carter became president. His Secretary of Defense, Dr. Harold Brown, had been head of defense research and Secretary of the Air Force under McNamara. On June 30, 1977, President Carter cancelled the B-1 program. Instead, he offered a program of further updating the B-52 force and deploying long-range cruise missiles in the strategic attack role.

The Air Force, shaken by the decision, responded with a program to upgrade the B-52 to carry cruise missiles, and began looking into bomber alternatives. The latter included development of a new aircraft for use as a cruise missile carrier, converting the F-111 tactical strike aircraft to the FB-111 configuration, "stretching" the existing FB-111s to improve their capabilities, and even building a new FB-111 variant. None of these proposals gained ground during the Carter Administration. Rather, a renewed interest in strategic bomber programs had to wait until Ronald Reagan took office as President in January 1981. The manned bomber had become an issue during the 1980 presidential campaign, as candidate Ronald Reagan demanded an increase in American defense spending. Then, on August 22, 1980, Secretary of Defense Brown announced that

---

38. In 1962 the US military aircraft designation system was revised, and the next bomber subsequent to the B-70 restarted the bomber series with the B-1.

the United States was in fact developing a new strategic bomber in secret, the so-called "stealth" aircraft. The aircraft would be essentially invisible to enemy radar as well as "other" means of detection.

There were immediate charges—mostly from Republican members of Congress and the press—that the Carter Administration had raised the stealth aircraft issue as a political ploy. Some also charged that in doing so Mr. Carter and Dr. Brown were revealing highly classified information. Obviously, work had long been underway—and incorporated into many aircraft—to reduce radar signatures, hot engine exhaust, and other features. J.W.R. Taylor in the 1977 edition of *Jane's All the World's Aircraft* wrote of how the Lockheed laboratory known as the "Skunk Works," which had given us the U-2 and SR-71 aircraft, was developing a new aircraft, "of which a primary feature is low radar, infra-red and optical signatures."

The Carter Administration's "damage" seems in retrospect to have been to provide a better focus for Soviet intelligence efforts. It also became evident that no specific stealth bomber production program was underway or planned. As the Reagan Administration took office, there was immediate interest in a new bomber program. The question, however, became *which* bomber: to restart the B-1 effort? to develop a B-1 derivative? or to begin development of a specific advanced technology aircraft? The improved FB-111 force could have been operational as early as 1984 (one squadron) while the first B-1 would be operational in 1986, with the entire 200-plane force in service by about 1990 at the earliest.

President Reagan's proposed strategic plan calls for retaining some 265 B-52G/H manned bombers and fitting them to carry the ALCM cruise missile (see below). The older B-52D aircraft would be retired in 1982–1983, with the 65 FB-111s being phased out a few years later.

More significantly, after the long hiatus in bomber production, President Reagan has proposed *two* bombers for production. Rockwell International will produce 100 of the B-1B variant of that long-in-development aircraft, with the first squadron scheduled to become operational in 1986. Although the cost of the B-1 (estimated in 1982 at some $200 to $300 million per plane) has soared, and some experts contend that it will be unable to penetrate Soviet air defenses by the late 1980s, the Reagan Administration made the B-1 decision to compensate for the delays in the M-X and Trident programs plus the Soviet buildup of strategic weapons. The B-1 also will serve primarily as a cruise missile aircraft, with the total B-52/B-1 force of 365 bombers being armed with some 3,000 ALCMs.

A "vigorous" R&D program for the Advanced Technology Bomber (ATB), or "Stealth" aircraft, also is planned. Northrop—whose last bomber effort was the B-49 Flying Wing—has been selected as the prime contractor for the Stealth bomber. The only announced schedule for the Stealth is deployment "in the 1990s," with some press reports citing a prototype flight in 1984. Defense Department officials estimate about $10 billion will be required for Stealth development, with unofficial sources placing a similar pricetag on a production run of 50 to 100 aircraft.

Questions have been raised in Congress about the two-track approach to strategic bomber development. The long delay in providing a replacement for the B-52 force and the near-term availability of the B-1 make that program appear viable. A Stealth production decision in the 1980s seems less likely, with an increase in B-1 production being an alternative consideration, at least during the 1980s.

The Tactical Aircraft

Although they are not generally considered in the context of strategic aircraft, the United States has tactical aircraft forward-based in Western Europe and South Korea, and forward-deployed aboard aircraft carriers, that can reach some portions of the Soviet Union with small, tactical nuclear weapons. The US Air Force currently flies the F-111 and F-4 Phantom fighters, which have a tactical nuclear capability. The former aircraft has a small, internal weapons bay, and the F-4 Phantom—flown by a number of Western nations as well as Israel and Iran—can be fitted to carry tactical nuclear weapons on external pylons.

The US Navy normally operates one or two large aircraft carriers in the Mediterranean and one or two in the western Pacific, each with some 70 to 90 aircraft. During crisis periods the number of carriers forward-deployed can be increased to a majority of the 12 large carriers in service. All of these ships have squadrons of A-6 Intruder and A-7 Corsair attack planes that can be configured for delivering tactical nuclear weapons. It is not publicly known at this writing how many aircraft or which type within the carrier air wings are rigged for nuclear weapons delivery. (The older concept of carrier-based "heavy attack" aircraft, developed through the AJ Savage, A3D Skywarrior, and A3J Vigilante, has been discarded in favor of smaller aircraft as the carrier's role in strategic warfare has been downgraded.)

In the late 1970s the US Air Force began replacing F-4 fighters with the F-15 Eagle and F-16 Fighting Falcon, neither of which is "wired" for nuclear weapon delivery. Similarly, during the 1980s the F/A-18 Hornet is planned to replace the A-7 in the light attack role aboard carriers, and initially at least will not have a nuclear weapon capability. This will leave the ten A-6E Intruders on each ship as the only nuclear-capable aircraft aboard carriers (with 14–15 carriers proposed for the 1990s).

Land-Based Missiles

The Strategic Air Command currently operates 1,000 Minuteman ICBMs, 550 of which carry the three-MIRV Minuteman-III configuration,[39] and 52 of the large Titan-II missiles. (See Figure 9-5.) These weapons are in partially protected underground silos in the central and western portions of the United States. They are solid-propellant ICBMs that can be launched on short notice to strike targets in the Soviet Union or mainland China with a flight time of less than 30 minutes.

These 1,052 ICBMs have a potential of delivering a total of 2,152 RVs against the Soviet Union. Most of these are small weapons, about 200-KT for each of the Minuteman-III reentry vehicles, and about one megaton for each Minuteman-II warhead. The 52 large Titan-II weapons each have a warhead of about 9-MT. Thus, the land-based ICBM force provides both a large number of RVs and, in the few Titan-II missiles, large warheads.

As indicated above, the Minuteman ICBM was a *series* rather than a single missile, with the Minuteman-III version becoming operational from 1970 onward. Further, in the early 1980s some 300 Minuteman-III missiles were to be refitted to carry the Mk 12A warhead, a three-MIRV warhead with each vehicle delivering an estimated 350-KT with improved accuracy. The Titan-II of the 1980s, however, is the same Titan-II that was deployed in 1961. At that time it had an intended service life of perhaps a decade. Now, two decades later, the missile, propelled by storable liquid fuel, remains in service. The missile's highly toxic fuel—nitrogen tetroxide—has caused several problems. In 1978 a fuel problem

---

39. In September 1974, Secretary Schlesinger approved the deployment of 50 additional Minuteman-III missiles; previously the Minuteman mix had been authorized at 550 Minuteman-III and 450 Minuteman-II missiles.

at a Titan-II in Rock, Kansas killed two airmen and sent 20 others to the hospital. The next publicized accident took place in September 1980, when a Titan-II near Damascus, Arkansas exploded while airmen were trying to repair a fuel problem. One man was killed and 21 were injured. The missile's 9-MT warhead was blown off the missile in the accident.

Although the Air Force had begun an improvement program for the Titan-II missiles, the Reagan Administration decided to dismantle the large ICBMs beginning in 1982.

The overage Titan-II ICBM was retained because it is the largest strategic missile in the US arsenal, with a launch weight of 330,000 pounds (more than four times larger than the Minuteman), while carrying nine times the megatonnage of the Minuteman II. While the Titan payload is a single RV, the size of that weapon makes it highly desirable for use against hardened Soviet targets, especially underground command centers. The United States has proposed that both sides dismantle heavy ICBMs, but the Soviet Union insisted on retaining the heavy SS-9 missile (25-MT yield with a single RV), and then replaced it with the similarly heavy MIRV-warhead SS-18 while also introducing the medium SS-17 and SS-19 ICBMs during the 1970s. With B-52 or FB-111 manned bombers the only other US strategic delivery system with a multi-megatonnage delivery capability, the Titan-II remained an important element of a versatile US strategic force through 1982.

The principal Soviet threat to the Minuteman-Titan ICBMs is the potential of a preemptive attack by Soviet land-based ICBMs against the US weapons while the latter are still in their underground silos. Soviet SLBMs—according to most Western estimates—lack the accuracy needed to zero in on the underground missile silos. During the 1960s it became evident that the Soviet Strategic Rocket Forces could become a threat to US missile survivability by a continued proliferation of ICBMs, by increases in accuracy, or by MIRV developments. Lieutenant General W. P. Leber, US Army, manager of one phase of the US ABM program in the mid-1970s, stated that even the Soviet ICBM inventory at the time with essentially single-warhead missiles ''with improvement of accuracy alone . . . could reduce Minuteman survivors to unacceptable levels.'' The subsequent Soviet improvements in accuracy and deployment of MIRV warheads from the mid-1970s onward in fact have made the US ICBMs vulnerable to a Soviet missile strike. In 1978, former Chief of Naval Operations Elmo R. Zumwalt estimated that the Soviets could soon be able to destroy over 90 percent of the American ICBMs with only 20 percent of the Soviet MIRVed ICBM force, given their new accuracies.

Possible U.S. defenses against this threat include further hardening of Minuteman-Titan silos, replacement of fixed ICBMs with mobile ICBM launchers on railway trains or motor trucks or other basing schemes, deployment of additional silo-based ICBMs, or installation of defensive ABM missiles. The SALT I agreements provided for a single Safeguard ABM site to defend 150 of the Minuteman missiles, but that facility was never finished. The defensive utility of the options of hardening and defensive missiles could be overcome by available technology (increased RV accuracy and increased RV numbers, respectively). Neither of these potential Soviet counterforce options regarding RVs were restricted by SALT I and, because they are qualitative rather than quantitative in nature, such aspects of weaponry are difficult to control.

A final factor in considering US Minuteman-Titan ICBM effectiveness is the question of reliability. Of the three components of the current TRIAD, the land-based ICBMs are the only force that has not been extensively tested. Bombers regularly take off, fly missions, and drop bombs; prior to test-ban agreements, bombers even dropped nuclear weapons. Similarly, submarines have regularly fired unarmed Polaris, Poseidon, and Trident missiles on test ranges; and on May 6, 1962, the USS *Ethan Allen* fired a Polaris A-1 missile almost 1,200 nautical miles in the Pacific with a nuclear detonation. No ICBM has been fired from an operational silo. Periodically, the silo crews have fired various ICBMs from test facilities at the Vandenberg Air Force Base in California under highly controlled conditions. Efforts to launch an "operational" ICBM with reduced fuel and no warhead from an operational silo have failed, and Congress has refused approval of full-range test firings from an operational silo that would take the missile over urban areas. (The Soviets regularly test missiles from both research facilities and operational missile sites, with flights across the Soviet Union to target ranges in Siberia or to the Pacific.)

During 1966-67, the Department of Defense conducted a technical study of future ballistic missiles. Known as the STRAT-X study, it recommended—from numerous candidate weapons—the development of four advanced strategic systems, two land-based and two sea-based. The land-based weapons were ICBMs in hard-rock silos and ground-mobile ICBMs; the sea-based systems were long-range missiles in advanced

Figure 9-6, Figure 9-7, Figure 9-8. Shown here is an advanced strategic weapons concept successfully tested by the U.S. Air Force in the fall of 1974. A Minuteman ICBM is pulled in its cradle from a Lockheed C-5A Galaxy transport by parachute, stabilized in midair, and then fired for a few seconds. The tests demonstrated the feasibility of launching large ballistic missiles from transport-type aircraft. This was one of the numerous launch schemes later considered for the MX missile to enhance its pre-launch survivability. (U.S. Air Force)

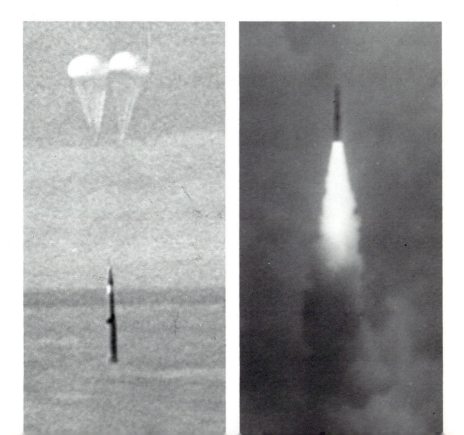

Figure 9-9. A number of land-mobile concepts for reducing the vulnerability of the next-generation ICBM were examined under the MX program. This 1978 photograph shows a test of the buried trench concept, wherein the missile was on a rail line in a shallow trench, partially exposed (for satellite verification under SALT) and partially covered. Here a dummy missile launcher breaks through the soft covering. (U.S. Air Force)

Figure 9-10. The U.S. nuclear-propelled attack submarine *Phoenix* had just been launched when this photograph was taken at the General Dynamics/Electric Boat yard in Groton, Connecticut, in December 1979. In the center is the giant Trident missile submarine *Michigan* and at the left, in the water, is the first Trident submarine, the *Ohio*. The bow of the third Trident submarine can be seen at the upper right, protruding from the covered building ways. (General Dynamics/Electric Boat)

Figure 9-11. A BGM-109 Tomahawk cruise missile streaks skyward from the submerged attack submarine *Guitarro*. Shortly after leaving the water the missile's stub wings, tail fins, and turbofan engine inlet will extend. The Tomahawk can be launched from the standard 21-inch diameter, 21-foot long torpedo tubes of attack or missile submarines. (U.S. Navy)

Figure 9-12, Figure 9-13, Figure 9-14. The Air-Launched Cruise Missile (ALCM) offers the potential for the first major change in American bomber strategy since the Billy Mitchell era of the early 1920s. These photographs show an AGM-86B ALCM with wings and tail extended; "packaged" for loading in a B-52 weapons bay; and being released in flight from a B-52G modified for ALCM tests. (U.S. Air Force)

Figure 9-15. The Navy's Tomahawk has also been proposed as a Ground-Launched Cruise Missile (GLCM) for employment as a theater nuclear weapon with NATO forces in Europe. This is a mock-up of the Transporter-Erector-Launcher (TEL) that would carry four Tomahawk GLCMs. The system would be operated by the U.S. Air Force or, under a joint control arrangement, by the Air Force and foreign military services. (U.S. Air Force)

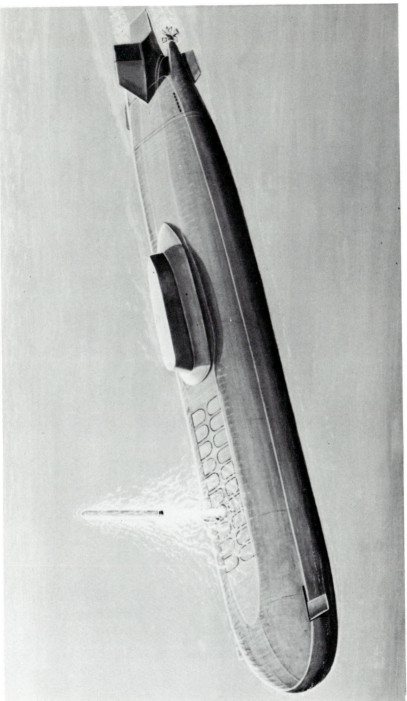

This is a US artist's portrayal of the Soviet Typhoon-class SLBM submarine. At some 25,000 tons, it is about half again as large as the American Trident submarine. Note that the 20 tubes for the SS-N-20 missile are *forward* of the sail structure and the twin-propeller configuration.

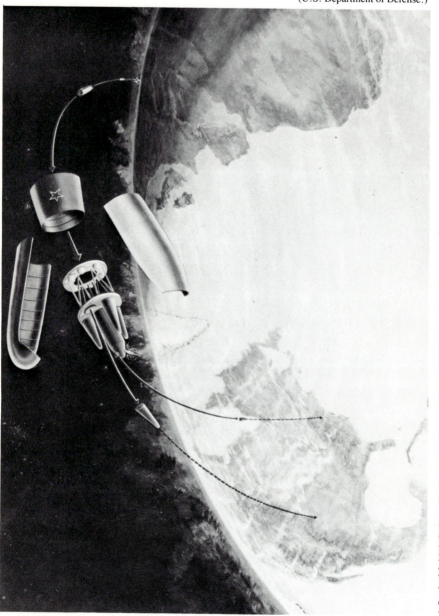

A Soviet Multiple Independently-targeted Reentry Vehicle (MIRVed) warhead begins to separate in this artist's view. Note that two Reentry Vehicles, aimed at the United States, have separated from the "bus" and that several more remain on the Post Boost Vehicle.

submarines (originally known as ULMS for Underwater Longrange Missile System), and a surface-ship missile system. Of the four specific systems proposed, only the ULMS concept survived; in modified form, it is the current Trident program.

Instead, US research and development efforts related to the ICBM force were concentrated in specific technology areas, among them the ABRES (Advanced Ballistic Reentry System) program, refinements in the existing Minuteman guidance system that could increase accuracy, development of higher-yield RVs for the Minuteman-III (designated Mk 12A), and research into providing the Minuteman-III with a larger number of small RVs (the Pave Pepper program). The Navy developed the Mk 500 Maneuvering Reentry Vehicle (MaRV) that could be compatible with both the Trident SLBM and the Minuteman ICBM. Another consideration for improving the effectiveness and survivability of ICBMs at the time was the airborne launch concept. During the fall of 1974, concrete slabs simulating a variety of missile weights, and then an 86,000-pound Minuteman-I missile, were test-dropped by parachute from huge C-5A transport aircraft. (See Figures 9-6, 9-7, and 9-8.) The Minuteman-I missile was ignited briefly to test its first-stage engine. The evaluation was technically successful. This concept, although more flexible and hence possibly more survivable than a fixed, land-based ICBM, would be considerably more expensive to maintain. Moreover, the air-launched ICBM can be assumed to have less accuracy than a land-based or sea-mobile ICBM.[40]

The M-X Program

By the mid-1970s the predicted threat to American ICBMs from the new Soviet strategic missiles reached the point that the Department of Defense consolidated various advanced ICBM-related technology research into the M-X project, intended to develop a new American ICBM with enhanced survivability over the existing Minuteman-Titan missiles. At an early stage missile mobility was looked at as the best means for

---

40. The concept of air-launching strategic missiles was previously examined by the US Air Force with the Rascal (13,000 lbs.), Skybolt (11,300 lbs.), Navaho (120,500 lbs.), and current SRAM missiles. An aircraft proposed in the late 1950s to carry two Navaho missiles on airborne alert, called the XC-Heavy, was so large that its landing gear track would have permitted it to use less than a dozen airfields in the world. An alternative payload for the XC-heavy would have been a single 160,000 pound B-58 bomber!

improving survivability and about 30 schemes were examined, including moving the missiles by train along rail track; moving the missiles on rail in buried trenches; carrying some missiles on airborne alert and launching them while aloft or as the missile aircraft touched down at pre-designated bases; moving the missiles by a wheeled vehicle among a large number of underground silos or to hardened, above-ground launch shelters; and a variety of other schemes. (See Figure 9-9.) Periodically proposals also were put forth to carry the M-X to sea, in large submarines, or surface ships, or even small, two-missile submersibles that could operate in protected, coastal waters.

In June of 1979, President Carter reluctantly approved full-scale development of the M-X missile—reluctantly because he had hoped that SALT II agreements with the USSR would preclude the need to develop the next generation of ICBMs. Tentative characteristics of the missile as then approved are shown below in comparison with the two Trident missiles.

MISSILE CHARACTERISTICS

	M-X	*TRIDENT-I (C-4)*	*TRIDENT-II (D-5)*
Weight	190,000 lbs	65,000 lbs	~126,000 lbs
Length	71 ft	34 ft	44 ft
Diameter	92 in	74 in	82 in
Throw weight	7,900 lbs		
Payload	10 Mk 12A	8 Mk-4	
Range	6,000 n.miles	4,000 n.miles	~6,000 n.miles
IOC	1986	1979	1989

In addition, the M-X would have considerably more accuracy than previous missiles, while delivering a payload of ten Mk 12A reentry vehicles targeted against separate points within the missile's "footprint."

During the development of the M-X it was proposed that the first two boosters and possibly the warhead of the M-X might be used as components of the new Trident SLBM. This proposal carried the benefits of economy in cost and provision of additional M-X basing options. However, it would have constrained the M-X to the planned 83-inch diameter missile tubes in Trident submarines and limited American options to one new strategic missile. Left unsaid was an Air Force fear of being forced to accept another Navy program, as has been the case with the F-4 Phantom and A-7 Corsair aircraft, both of which were developed for naval use and were subsequently forced on the Air Force as well.

Ground mobility became the key to the M-X, and in September 1979 President Carter chose the so-called "racetrack" deployment plan. Under this plan each M-X would be transported by a large vehicle on a closed-loop road network with 23 shelters. The missile transporter, a vehicle weighing some 700,000 pounds when carrying a missile and 180 feet long, would operate only on the road network. Periodically the missile would shift from one shelter to another, meaning that satellite targeting by the Soviets would have limited value. The missile could be launched from the vehicle on the roadway or from one of the 23 hardened shelters.

Thus, the M-X program would provide 200 missiles on the 200 road networks with some 4,600 shelters. To be built in southwestern states, the M-X bases would have the advantages of survivability and verification. Satellites would record one missile moving onto each road network and then the road would be blocked, so that no additional missiles could enter a given 23-shelter network. To insure killing all missiles, the Soviets in theory would have to destroy all 4,600 shelters.

Problems and opposition quickly arose, however. First, critics pointed out that moving an ICBM regularly, even on a special transporter and on special roads, would create major problems because of vibration, and periodically loading and unloading the missile into the shelters would cause other problems. More significant, politically at least, was the fact that the two states chosen for M-X deployment, Utah and Nevada, both objected to the deployment. Indeed, even the words being used to describe it ran afoul of politicians and the public. The "racetrack" term was soon dropped, as was the acronym MAPS for Multiple Aim Point System, the latter after one Air Force general called the scheme a "sponge" with the thousands of shelters "soaking up" Soviet nuclear weapons. Subsequently MPS for "Multiple Protective Shelters" was adopted.

Opposition in Congress and the press reflected general dissatisfaction with the M-X concept as the Carter-Brown Administration and the Air Force sought to gain backing on Capitol Hill. The Air Force in 1980 published its schedule for M-X: first flight in 1983, initial operational capability of ten missiles in 1986, and full capability with 200 missiles in 1989. At that time the Titan-II missiles—*if* they still existed—would be almost 30 years old, and the newer Minuteman-III missiles about half that age. Furthermore the ICBM "leg" of the TRIAD, assuming that concept was still the basis of American strategic force planning, would consist of only 200 missiles and 2,000 warheads. However, survivability and improved accuracy could compensate for the reduction in numbers of missiles and warheads.

As the Reagan Administration took office in early 1981, confusion over the M-X deployment mode continued. One astute observer commented that never had a strategic system been the subject of so much analysis yet evoked so little confidence. Several alternative deployments were immediately considered by the new Administration. Of particular significance, some defense experts proposed a fixed-silo M-X with an ABM system deployed to defend the missiles against preemptive Soviet attack. This proposal, in turn, helped to spur new interest in ballistic missile defenses. The Army's Ballistic Missile Defense Systems Command put forth a plan for a two-tiered layered defense, with both high-altitude intercept missiles (exoatmospheric, or above 300,000 feet) and a low-altitude intercept system (under 200,000 feet). The high-altitude system would be based on new technology developments, while the second phase would employ an upgraded version of the Sprint interceptor of the Sentinal/Safeguard ABM period. The latter would have a 15-second or less detection-to-intercept time span, demonstrating the complexities of ballistic missile defense.

At the other end of the spectrum of M-X deployment proposals that came forth in 1980-81 was the concept of moving the M-X to sea, either in small submarines, perhaps carrying as few as two or four ICBMs, or in large, merchant-type surface ships. Both schemes suffer from limitations, especially the small submarines because of their high cost on a per-missile basis and the high risk of collisions with civilian shipping in the coastal waters where they would operate. (Shipping problems—as well as political considerations—also prevent the submarines being placed on the Great Lakes, as some persons have suggested.) While putting the M-X to sea in merchant ships would involve some degree of vulnerability, it is an inexpensive and short lead-time option. Here U.S. inter-service problems could lead to the ships being placed under Air Force operational control. While several Soviet surveillance systems would be able to detect the ships on a periodic basis, astute operating procedures, such as using acoustic decoys at night and operating in major shipping lanes, could inhibit continuous Soviet surveillance. Additionally, as the ships would be moving when at sea, pre-targeting would be difficult.

In late 1981 the Reagan Administration announced that it would undertake an ICBM modernization program that consists of deploying at least 100 M-X missiles as soon as possible, using existing Minuteman and Titan silos. The first ten M-X missiles would be emplaced in late 1986. In addition, R&D was to continue on three alternatives for long-term M-X basing: continuous airborne alert, deep underground basing, and active ABM defense of the missiles. Of these, the continuous airborne alert seems the least likely to be adopted because of cost, the public fear of an M-X aircraft crashing, and the communications problems involved with aircraft in a nuclear attack environment. The deep underground basing option has major problems associated with cost and even survival, in view of the size and quantity of Soviet ICBM warheads. Thus, the most likely long-term M-X deployment, if one beyond utilization of the existing ICBM silos is adopted, is the use of an ABM system to intercept a limited number of attacking warheads.

The multiple shelter and sea-base concepts have been discarded by the Reagan Administration. In describing the new M-X program, considerable effort was made by the Reagan staff to explain the problems accompanying the multiple shelter concept without mention of the maritime alternatives—small submarine, large nuclear submarine, or surface ship. The small M-X procurement coupled with the fact that the program is behind both the Trident submarine and B-1 bomber in schedule leaves open the possibility of further revisions in the missile's procurement and deployment plans, or its total cancellation.

Submarine-Launched Missiles

The third component of the current TRIAD to be deployed was the Submarine-Launched Ballistic Missile (SLBM) force, which in 1982 consisted of 31 older submarines, each armed with 16 Poseidon or Trident-I (C-4) missiles, plus the first of the new Trident submarines, the USS *Ohio,* with 24 Trident-I SLBMs. Ten earlier Polaris missile submarines were decommissioned or converted to non-missile attack submarines in 1980–82.

After 20 years of intensive operation these ten submarines were worn out while their MRV Polaris A-3 missiles were of limited importance in view of almost 5,000 MIRV warheads available in the 31 Poseidon sub-

marines (some subsequently converted to fire the Trident-I missile). However, for political reasons, largely at the urgings of Admiral H. G. Rickover, head of the nuclear propulsion program, the Navy was forced to
keep the Polaris submarines in service until 1980–82, each with two
crews of some 140 men; this required some 3,000 men, all highly trained
and more than half in difficult-to-retain nuclear fields.

Thus, in mid-1982 there were 31 American SLBM submarines in service. At any given time, just over half of these submarines were at sea
with their missiles in a very high degree of readiness.[41] Any major threat
to the Polaris-Poseidon SLBM force that may emerge would probably
come from Soviet Anti-Submarine Warfare (ASW) forces. Soviet fleet
development has been multifaceted, and includes both offensive and defensive components. Certain ships—such as the large, graceful, and heavily armed helicopter ships *Moskva* and *Leningrad,* the nuclear-
propelled torpedo-attack submarines, and the computer-equipped Il-38
May ASW aircraft—probably were developed for anti-Polaris/Poseidon
operations. However, Soviet ASW capabilities are one of the more difficult aspects of Soviet military power to understand. For example, the
Soviet Navy has not pursued the development of large surface-ship sonars,
as the US Navy has done. On the other hand, there is evidence that the
Soviets are investigating such diverse aspects of ASW as satellite and
psychic detection, and the possibility was at one point suggested that the
Yankee/SS-N-13 system had an anti-submarine role.

Most authorities appear to agree that Soviet ASW is not now, and will
not be for the near future, capable of destroying a significant portion of
the missile submarine force. Senior defense officials rarely speak in terms
of absolute effectiveness or the absolute survivability of any one strategic
weapon. Yet, in 1970, Secretary of Defense Laird did state that:

> According to our best current estimates, we believe that our Polaris
> and Poseidon submarines at sea can be considered virtually invulnerable
> today. With a highly concentrated effort, the Soviet Navy today might
> be able to localize and destroy at sea one or two Polaris submarines.
> But the massive and expensive undertaking that would be required to

---

41. In these calculations the Polaris A-3 is considered as a single weapon, although
actually three MRVs are aimed at the same target. US Navy SLBM submarines normally
are at sea for 60 days and in port for 30 days; the number of submarines normally at sea
is less than two thirds of the force, however, because of submarines in overhaul (including
nuclear refueling), training, missile tests, and so forth.

extend such a capability using any currently known ASW techniques would take time and would certainly be evident.

Three factors probably will reduce SLBM effectiveness in the future: Soviet ASW efforts, the aging of US submarines, and the reduced number of submarines. In this regard, Secretary Laird's 1970 statement also noted:

> However, a combination of technological development, and the decision by the Soviets to undertake a worldwide ASW effort, might result in some increased degree of Polaris/Poseidon vulnerability beyond the mid-1970s. I would hope that Polaris would remain invulnerable at least through the 1970s. But, as a defense planner, I would never guarantee the invulnerability of *any* strategic system beyond the reasonably foreseeable future, say five to seven years.

With respect to aging, the Navy's 41 missile submarines were completed during the years 1960 to 1967; by 1980, the oldest submarines had undergone 20 years of high-tempo operations. In time, submarine machinery noise levels increase, while at the same time ASW detection capabilities improve. Moreover, the ships simply wear out after 20 to 30 years of operation. These factors led to the STRAT-X study of 1966-67, which recommended two advanced sea-based strategic missile systems, one surface and one submarine; the latter was the Undersea Long-range Missile System (ULMS). Subsequently approved for development as the Trident SLBM, the system provides for an advanced submarine with improved quieting and other features not available in the older Polaris-Poseidon undersea craft, and an advanced, multi-warhead missile with a range of about 6,000 nautical miles. With that missile range, a Trident SLBM submarine could cruise in the western Atlantic or western Pacific oceans and still have Moscow within range of its weapons. These ocean-wide operating areas would make most Soviet ASW efforts, of whatever nature, more difficult than ASW efforts against Polaris-Poseidon submarines, which have a maximum missile range of about 2,500 nautical miles.

The surface missile ship proposal was not approved for development. Periodically, the Navy has studied the feasibility of installing strategic missiles on surface ships, both warships and merchant-type ships. The Surface Launched Missile System (SLMS) of the STRAT-X study and Ballistic Missile Ship (BMS) concepts provide for either IRBMs, such as the Polaris or Poseidon, or longer-range Minuteman ICBMs to be installed in fast (20- to 30-knot) merchant ships. Having the superficial appearance of commercial cargo ships, the missile-armed merchantmen could operate in world shipping lanes, and would require large increases in Soviet countermeasures.[42] Studies have indicated that shifting Minuteman ICBMs from underground silos to modular launchers in merchant-type ships would significantly increase their survivability from Soviet preemptive attacks and would also enable the missiles to target the Soviet Union from any broad ocean area. Nevertheless, the SLMS/BMS option was deferred.

On the other hand, the ULMS/Trident program was initiated. In early 1972, Secretary Laird told the Congress that: "I have carefully reviewed all alternatives for new strategic initiatives, and have decided that acceleration of the ULMS program is the most appropriate alternative, since the at-sea portion of our sea-based strategic forces has the best long-term prospect for pre-launch survivability."

The original STRAT-X proposal had called for a relatively small SLBM submarine (i.e., slightly larger than the existing Polaris-Poseidon craft), with a slow speed (perhaps 20 knots maximum), carrying a missile with a range of some 6,000 nautical miles. In an effort to obtain maximum support from Admiral Rickover, head of the nuclear propulsion program, the Chief of Naval Operations, Admiral Elmo R. Zumwalt, accepted a much larger submarine design to accommodate a new, large reactor plant. At the same time, an "interim" Trident-I missile was accepted with a range of 4,000 nautical miles and a maximum payload of eight MIRV warheads of some 40-KT each.

Further, acceptance of the lesser-range missile meant that it could be fitted into some of the existing Polaris-Poseidon submarines. Thus, the Trident program would actually have three phases:

- fitting of the Trident-I SLBM in 12 existing submarines
- construction of a new class of very large missile submarines (18,700 tons submerged displacement)
- development of the longer-range Trident-II missile for fitting in the new submarines (which could also fire the Trident-I)

---

42. Although satellites could detect the ships quite easily, they could not necessarily distinguish whether the ship was a missile ship or commercial ship. More important, a preemptive future strike would be difficult to plan because the ships at sea would always be moving.

The first phase, development of the 4,000 nautical-mile Trident I, went well, in part because it was a further refinement of the Polaris/Poseidon series. Starting in 1979, the 12 latest Poseidon submarines were rearmed with that improved missile. At the same time, however, development of the originally proposed 6,000 nautical-mile Trident-II was postponed indefinitely by the Carter Administration. In its balanced approach to US strategic force development, the Reagan Administration announced plans to develop and, beginning in 1989, to deploy the Trident-II missile, and to continue the construction of the giant, 18,700-ton Trident submarines.

The real bottleneck of the Trident-I program was the giant SLBM submarines, each of which was to have 24 missile tubes, half-again as many as previous missile submarines. (See Figure 9-10.) The lead submarine—the USS *Ohio*—was funded by Congress in the fiscal 1974 shipbuilding program. The Navy had planned to start three more ships every year for an initial batch of ten. The lead ship was to be completed in 1979 (although, at Admiral Rickover's insistence, a clause was inserted in the contract that the shipyard would make every effort to finish the submarine by December 1977).

Construction of the Trident submarines was soon far behind schedule; major problems in the shipyard, in the Navy's management of the project, and in Navy-shipyard liaison were devastating. The completion date of the *Ohio* slipped and the costs of the Trident program skyrocketed, ably abetted by the nation's soaring inflation. Completion schedules were constantly revised, and it became apparent that the *Ohio* would not be completed until 1982, having taken almost twice as long to build as originally planned. At the same time, the later Trident submarines had a 1980 pricetag of about $1.5 *billion* per submarine (without missiles). The Trident submarine delays led to a decline of the American SLBM force which took effect from 1980 onward.

With the existing Trident construction rate and delays, by about 1995—when the last of the older submarines will have been retired—there will be a US force of perhaps 17 submarines with 408 missiles. While improved, multiple warheads and the longer-range Trident-II (D-5) strategic missiles should then be available, the small number of submarines that could be kept on station would increase the potential danger from Soviet ASW efforts.

On several occasions Defense and Navy officials have sought to start smaller Trident submarines—undersea craft that would have smaller propulsion plants and possibly fewer missiles (most likely 16 or 20, although possibly 24), but could be constructed at a more rapid rate and less cost than the giants of the *Ohio* class. These efforts were still-born, largely because of the opposition of Admiral Rickover to smaller designs. His forced retirement in January 1982 after more than three decades in charge of the Navy's nuclear propulsion program could lead to a reopening of consideration of this option.

Still another submarine missile alternative proposed in the late 1970s was the Shallow Underwater Mobile (SUM) system. Proposed by several strategic analysts, this submarine would be about 120 feet long and carry four Trident or M-X missiles external to the pressure hull. Conventional (diesel-electric) propulsion and a small crew would make the SUM relatively inexpensive to build and operate. The SUM submersibles would operate in the US coastal waters. However, Defense Department experts estimated that a 1,500-ton submarine would be the smallest craft suitable for the SUM concept, and that the smaller submersibles would be vulnerable to the underwater effects of offshore nuclear explosions. Other potential problems included support costs for a large fleet of small submersibles, command and control, and the problems of operating such small craft on long-duration patrols on a continuous basis.

The significance of SLBM submarines to the US strategic forces is generally based on the difficulty of detecting and attacking a slow-moving, quiet missile submarine on mid-ocean patrol. Most authorities agree that in the 1980s, in terms of vulnerability to Soviet defensive measures, the manned bomber is the most vulnerable strategic component and the SLBM submarine the least vulnerable. However, these considerations are not absolutes, and other factors should be considered. For example, Secretary

STRATEGIC FORCE CHARACTERISTICS

	ICBMs	*SLBMs*	*Bombers/ALCM*
Secure and Reliable C³	yes	?	?
Flexibility/Responsiveness	yes	?	no
Assured Penetration	yes	yes	?
Prompt Counterforce	yes	?	no
Sovereign Basing	yes	no	yes
Enduring Survivability	?	yes	?
Survives Without Tactical Warning	?	yes	no

of Defense Brown in 1979 presented the strategic force "characteristics" set forth in the preceding chart as summarizing his view of the relative vulnerabilities and effectiveness of US strategic systems. These categories and judgments are not indubitable, but are illustrative of one method of deciding on alternative strategic offensive systems. For example, is sovereign basing a valid consideration when the seas are available to US submarine operations? Or, can advanced submarine communications systems, such as lasers and radio relay aircraft, or extensive ground systems, such as Sanguine, provide secure and reliable command, control, and communications?

Cruise Missiles—Again

The US Navy abandoned the Regulus cruise missile in favor of the Polaris ballistic missile for the land-attack role in the late 1950s. More than a decade later, during the tenure of Admiral Zumwalt as CNO (1970-74), the US Navy developed a renewed interest in *tactical* cruise missiles for the anti-ship role, first the 60 nautical-mile Harpoon and then the longer-range Tomahawk. The latter missile—some 18½ feet long and 21 inches in diameter to permit firing from submarine torpedo tubes—has the capability of delivering small nuclear warheads over distances of two thousand miles or more.

Cruise missiles, and especially the Tomahawk, are versatile weapons which within a few years could be deployed extensively. Of particular significance, Tomahawk could permit the rapid deployment of long-range nuclear attack missiles aboard any forward-deployed submarines (torpedo-attack as well as SLBM submarines) and surface warships—although, because of its slow speed (about Mach 0.8), it is not an effective first-strike weapon. (See Figure 9-11.). Also, cruise missiles are "cheap," costing on the order of $1 million each (without the warhead), as compared to much higher costs for ballistic missiles and their launching systems.

However, there are several limitations in, or at least questions about, the cruise missile in the long-range nuclear attack role. These include:

Confidence. Once a ballistic missile is launched there can be a high degree of confidence that the warhead(s) will strike the target(s) within a few minutes. A cruise missile after launching is many complex evolutions and hours of flight time from hitting its target. This factor of confidence is an important consideration in strategic planning.

Threats. Cruise missiles will be vulnerable to advanced Soviet defenses. Although capable of flying considerably lower than can a bomber, and characterized by a significantly smaller radar cross section and heat signature, the cruise missile can be shot down by some surface-to-air missiles, advanced anti-aircraft guns, and fighters with lookdown radar. Also, wind and other adverse weather conditions can diminish cruise missile accuracy.

The question of cruise missile vulnerability became a political issue late in 1977 when it was decided to cancel a proposed "live" test of U.S. Hawk anti-aircraft missiles against a low-flying Tomahawk. Reportedly, computer studies had shown that the Hawk system could intercept the cruise missile. A "technical expert" has been quoted as telling Washington political columnists that "the cruise missile is about one weapon generation away from being able to penetrate Soviet defenses."

Overflights. The speeds, altitudes, and flight paths of ballistic missiles reduce or alleviate the problems of flying weapons through third nations' air space in attacking Soviet targets. The slow, low-flying cruise missile is more visible and hence more of a political problem, especially in launches from submarines or surface ships in the Norwegian Sea, the Mediterranean, or the Western Pacific.

Basing. Deployment of a sea-based strategic cruise missile will create a number of questions for the Navy. For example, if such weapons are deployed aboard attack submarines will the submarines lose operational flexibility? Will they be unable to shift patrol areas, or will there be restrictions on their making attacks against enemy shipping, before launching their Sea-Launched Cruise Missiles (SLCMs)? How would carrying such weapons aboard surface ships or submarines inhibit port visits? If cruise missiles were provided in Poseidon submarines, would the launching of a SLCM before the SLBMs are fired compromise the submarines' location? Is there any value in firing SLCMs from a Poseidon submarine *after* the SLBMs are launched?

Arms Limitation. Cruise missiles can also complicate the Strategic Arms Limitation Talks, which have a very high priority for the U.S. government. The principal problem that they present for SALT is verification. It is too difficult to ascertain if a Tomahawk cruise missile aboard a ship is a 300-mile or a 2,000-mile weapon. Indeed, how is an outsider to know whether the weapons in a torpedo-attack submarine's tubes and reload spaces are torpedoes, mines, or long-range SLCMs?

The SALT negotiations have included a proposal to limit cruise missile development initially to weapons with a range of 600 kilometers (300 nautical miles). This would mean that an Air-Launched Cruise Missile (ALCM) or SLCM launched from the Norwegian Sea could not even reach Leningrad, let alone inland targets. (At the same time, Soviet SLCMs of no greater range fired from 100 miles off the U.S. coast could strike most U.S. population and industrial centers.) Thus, the asymmetry of U.S. and Soviet geography coupled with SALT efforts to attain symmetrical weapon constraints is a major problem in cruise missile considerations.

The cruise missile, with its strategic potential, was adopted by the Carter-Brown Administration as an alternative to production of the B-1 advanced strategic bomber. The Tomahawk is capable of being launched from submarines, surface ships, and aircraft, as well as from land vehicles in a configuration known as GLCM (for Ground-Launched Cruise Missile). The air-launched Tomahawk was evaluated by the US Air Force for use from B-52G/H bombers in competition with another weapon for the ALCM role, with the latter weapon—the AGM-86B ALCM—being declared the winner in 1980. (See Figures 9-12 through 9-15.)

After examining several alternative aircraft to carry the ALCM, Secretary of Defense Brown decided on a program to modify the venerable B-52G/H aircraft to serve into the 1990s armed with ALCMs that would be launched against Soviet targets from distances of some 2,000 miles. This development—over 40 years after World War II and the introduction of effective air-to-surface missiles—would replace the gravity bomb as the principal weapon of the US strategic bomber force. Significantly, those B-52s that survived into the 1990s would be over 30 years old—possibly a record for combat aircraft longevity by a major power. ALCMs will also be carried by the B-1B and possibly by the Stealth (ATB) aircraft.

Still undecided in 1982 was the extent to which the Tomahawk Land-Attack Missile (T-LAM) would be deployed in US Navy torpedo-attack submarines. Fitted with either nuclear or 1,000-pound conventional warheads, the T-LAM could be launched from submarines in the Norwegian, Mediterranean, or Barents Seas to strike targets within the Soviet Union. Indeed, this development could make "conventional" cruise missiles a "strategic" weapon, in that they could strike the enemy's homeland with their range of approximately 2,000 miles.

Similarly, during the Carter Administration the decision was made to update the US theater nuclear weapons in Europe. These weapons are assigned to the NATO command, but are under US control. The "parity" of the US and Soviet Union in strategic weapons, the large Soviet deployment of SS-20 missiles, and the increasing obsolescence of US theater nuclear weapons led to the decision to deploy a Ground-Launched Cruise Missile (GLCM) and a new ballistic missile. The ranges of the new US theater weapons led to a new "linkage" of theater and strategic weapons. The current program calls for 464 Tomahawks to be deployed in the GLCM configuration mounted on four-tube truck launchers, plus 108 Pershing-II ballistic missiles. This program has been endorsed by the Reagan Administration.

While GLCMs provide a politically viable theater weapon by their being placed on European soil, use of the submarine T-LAM, deployed on NATO submarines with US personnel on board to control the missile warheads, could have involved a broader range of NATO nations in the use of theater nuclear weapons—or, indeed, offered more nations a role in NATO's strategic weapons capability. (The latter is now the exclusive province of the United States, Great Britain, and France [which, of course, is semi-estranged from NATO].) The GLCMs, and Pershing-IIs, while technically considered theater nuclear forces, could strike targets in the Soviet Union from positions in Britain and on the continent.

Thus, the "line" between strategic and theater nuclear weapons blurs. Perhaps new nomenclature is needed for "strategic" weapons. Even more urgent in the consideration of US nuclear weapons is recognition that the term TRIAD, coined after the fact to help justify continued development of ICBMs, missile submarines, and manned bombers, is outdated and should be discarded, so that it will not inhibit future development and thinking with respect to strategic weapons.

10

And Tomorrow

The development of strategic weapons—weapons of mass destruction that can strike an enemy's homeland—has continued in the nuclear era at a rapid pace, and continues today. The reasons for the development and for the evolution of specific weapons are complex issues. The preceding pages have sought to provide a brief overview of this evolution.

While the strategic weapons which will characterize the 1980s for the most part have been developed and already are deployed, the rate of weapons development may increase in the future. Also, new technologies—among them lasers and space-related systems—will undoubtedly be applied to strategic weapons. The Soviet efforts in the area of FOBS and anti-satellite systems were but the harbingers of future space-related systems.

In this regard, no Americans flew in space from 1975—when the United States joined the USSR in a joint space mission—until 1981. During that same period the Soviets flew a score of manned missions, with up to three Cosmonauts per mission; in so doing, the Soviets occupied a space laboratory and kept men in space for up to 185 consecutive days. During 1980 alone the Soviet Union undertook seven times the number of space launches as did the United States—89 compared to 13. (From the launch of Sputnik-1 on October 4, 1957 until the end of 1980, the Soviets logged 1,339 launches in which a payload achieved at least earth orbit; there were 587 similar US launches during the same period.) During just the

US-SOVIET STRATEGIC FORCES
(1982)

	United States	Soviet Union
ICBM Launchers	1,052	1,398
Long-Range Bombers[43]	347	156
Medium-Range Bombers[44]	65	600 +
Modern SLBM Launchers	496	950
Older SLBM Launchers	0	75
Modern SLBM Submarines	31	62
Older SLBM Submarines	0	25
Total Warheads	9,000	6,000
Anti-aircraft Missile Launchers	0	10,000
ABM Launchers	0	32
Air Defense Interceptors	300	2,600

period December 16 to 26, 1980, the Soviets had 12 space launches—two for the purpose of military photo reconnaissance, eight with military communications payloads (with eight satellites constituting one of those payloads), and two carrying television relay and scientific payloads. Also significant was the April 1980 testing by the Soviet Union, after a two-year hiatus, of its anti-satellite system. In this test, after being launched and completing one earth orbit, the Kosmos 1174 satellite intercepted the Kosmos 1171 launched earlier. While the US space shuttles are more sophisticated than the Soviet spacecraft, and the now-destroyed US Skylab was more sophisticated than the Soviet space lab, the Soviets have in fact done many space experiments and tests that America plans, or at some point wanted to plan.

The same may be said in the realm of strategic weapons. American weapons *may* be more sophisticated on a weapon-by-weapon comparison, but the USSR has deployed more weapons—of improving capabilities—in most categories, as well as some weapons that the United States has not even developed. The American B-1 has been cancelled, reborn, delayed, cancelled, resurrected; the M-X has been a confused, politically oriented effort; and the Trident submarine has been delayed almost beyond

---

43. US B-52; Soviet Tu-20 Bear, Mya-4 Bison (naval aircraft not included).
44. US FB-111; Soviet Tu-16 Badger, Tu-22 Blinder, Tu-22M Backfire (naval aircraft not included).

comprehension. By contrast, the Soviets have continued to regularly introduce new generations of their strategic weapons. To be certain, the Soviets have severe limitations and have encountered problems in their strategic weapons. However, their multi-track development efforts in several fields, coupled with early production decisions and large production runs, have compensated for such shortfalls.

The implications for the future are considerable.

APPENDIX A
Strategic Bomber Aircraft (1982)

Number Operational	Designation	IOC*	Gross Weight	Engines[a]	Maximum Speed	Crew	Notes
United States							
79[b]	B-52D Stratofortress	1956	450,000 lbs	6 TJ	633 mph	6	4 nuclear or 50,000 lbs conventional bombs.
172	B-52G Stratofortress	1958	488,000 lbs	6 TJ	633 mph	6	2 nuclear gravity bombs + 20 SRAMs.
96	B-52H Stratofortress	1961	488,000 lbs	6 TF	631 mph	6	2 nuclear gravity bombs + 20 SRAMs.
65	FB-111A	1968	114,300 lbs	2 TF	Mach 2.2	2	6 nuclear gravity bombs or 6 SRAMs.
Soviet Union[c]							
49	Mya-4 Bison-C[d]	1964?	350,000 lbs	4 TJ	560 mph	6–8	being phased out.
320	Tu-16 Badger-G[d]	1965	158,730 lbs	2 TJ	616 mph	7	medium bomber; carries 2 AS-5/6.
100	Tu-20 Bear-B[d]	1962	340,000 lbs	4 TP	500 mph	6–8	~75 carry 1 AS-3; design bureau designation Tu-95.**
140	Tu-22 Blinder-B[d]	1967	185,000 lbs	4 TJ	Mach 1.4	3	carries 1 AS-4.
70	Tu-22M Backfire-B	1974	270,000 lbs	2 TF	Mach 2	4?	carries 2 AS-4.
Great Britain							
48	Vulcan-B-2	1960	200,000 lbs	4 TJ	645 mph	5	nuclear or 21,000 lbs conventional bombs; being phased out.
France							
33	Mirage-IVA[e]	1964	73,800 lbs	2 TJ	Mach 2.2	2	1×50-KT bomb or 16,000 lbs conventional bombs.

[a] TJ = Turbojet; TP = Turboprop; TF = Turbofan.
[b] 180 additional B-52s of various marks in storage and test status.
[c] Does not include naval, reconnaissance, tanker, or test aircraft.
[d] Latest variant in service; some earlier aircraft may also be operational.
[e] A few additional aircraft are in storage.
* IOC = Initial Operational Capability.
** ~ = Approximately.

APPENDIX B
Ballistic Missiles (1982)

Number Operational	Designation		IOC	Launch Weight	Length	Engines[a]	Range (n.mi)	Warhead/Notes
United States								
52	LGM-25C Titan-II		1963	330,000 lbs	103 ft	R-L	8,100	1 RV × 9 MT; phasing out
450	LGM-30F Minuteman-III		1965	70,000 lbs	59⅔ ft	R-S	6,000	1 RV × 1–2 MT
550	LGM-30G Minuteman-III		1970	76,058 lbs	59⅔ ft	R-S	7,000	3 MIRV × 200 KT; 300 being converted to Mk 12A warhead from 1981 onward (3 MIRV × 350 KT)
Soviet Union[b]								
500+	SS-11 Sego	Mod 1	1966	~105,000 lbs	~62⅓ ft	R-L	7,500	1 RV × 1–2 MT
		Mod 2	1973					1 RV plus penetration aides
		Mod 3	1973					3 MRV × 100–300 KT
50	SS-13 Savage		1969	~77,000 lbs	~65 ft	R-S	4,320	1 RV × 1 MT
(not deployed)	SS-16		(1975)	~80,000 lbs	~65 ft	R-S	5,200	1 RV; land-mobile?
~150	SS-17	Mod 1	1975	~143,000 lbs	~80 ft	R-L	5,400	4 MIRV × 900 KT
		Mod 2					5,900	1 RV × ~5 MT

300+	SS-18	Mod 1	1974	~485,000 lbs	~120 ft	R-L	6,450	1 RV × 18–25 MT
		Mod 2	1975				5,900	8/10 MIRV × ~2 MT
		Mod 3					8,625	1 RV × 18–25 MT
		Mod 4						10 MIRV × 500 KT
300	SS-19	Mod 1	1975	~172,000 lbs	~90 ft	R-L	5,175	6 MIRV × 1–2 MT
		Mod 2					5,400	1 RV × ~5 MT
250	SS-20		1977	~28,500 lbs	~120 ft	R-S	3,100	IRBM; 3 MIRV × 150 KT; landmobile
~380	SS-4 Sandal	R-L	1959	~62,000 lbs	73½ ft		975	MRBM; 1 RV × 1 MT
~65	SS-5 Skean	R-L	1964	~132,000 lbs	~82 ft		1,900	IRBM; 1 RV × 1 MT
France								
9	S-2	R-S	1971	70,500 lbs	48½ ft		1,500	IRBM; 1 RV × 150 KT; to be replaced by S-3
9	S-3	R-S	1980	56,900 lbs	45 ft		1,900	IRBM; 1 RV × 1.2 MT
China								
50–90	CSS-1	R-L	early 1970s				540	MRBM; 1 RV
15–20	CSS-2	R-L	1970s				1,350	IRBM; 1 RV
few?	CSS-3	R-L	1970s				3,775	ICBM; 1 RV
few?	CSS-4	R-L	early 1980s	~400,000 lbs			5,400	ICBM; 1 RV × 3 MT?

ᵃ R = Rocket; L = Storable Liquid; S = Solid.

ᵇ US-NATO designations are given; Soviet designations are RS-16 (SS-17), RS-20 (SS-18), RS-18 (SS-19).

APPENDIX C
Submarine-Launched Ballistic Missiles (1982)

Submarines[a]	Missile Designation	IOC	Launch Weight	Length	Engines[b]	Range (n.mi)	Warhead/Notes
United States							
25 *Lafayette*	UGM-73 Poseidon C-3	1971	65,000 lbs	34 ft	R-S	~2,000[c]	8/10 MIRV × ~40 KT; being replaced by Trident C-4 in 6 submarines.
6 *Lafayette*	UGM-73A Trident C-4	1979	65,000 lbs	34 ft	R-S	4,000	8 MIRV
(10) *Ohio[d]*							
(10) *Ohio[d]*	Trident D-5	(1989)	~126,000 lbs	44 ft	R-S	~6,000	MIRV
Great Britain							
4 *Resolution*	Polaris A-3	1964	36,000 lbs	32$\frac{1}{3}$ ft	R-S	2,500	3 MRV × 200 KT
Soviet Union[e]							
3 Golf-I	SS-N-4 Sark	1958	~44,000 lbs	~49 ft	R-L	350	1 RV × ~1 MT; surface launch
13 Golf-II	SS-N-5 Serb	1963	~37,000 lbs	~43 ft	R-L	700	1 RV × ~1 MT; underwater launch
7 Hotel-II							

1 Golf-IV } few Yankee }	SS-N-6 Mod 1 Mod 2 Mod 3	1968 1974 1974	~42,000 lbs	~33 ft	R-L	1,300 1,600 1,600	1 RV × 1 MT 1 RV × 1 MT 2 MRV
1 Golf-III 1 Hotel-III } 19 Delta-I } 4 Delta-II	SS-N-8	1973		~43 ft	R-L	4,200	1 RV × 1–1.5 MT
? Yankee-II 1 Yankee-III	SS-N-16 SS-N-17	1970s 1970s		~35 ft	R-S	1,600– 2,150	(possibly version of SS-N-6) 1 RV × ~1 MT; improved accuracy
several Delta-III	SS-N-18 Mod 1 Mod 2 Mod 3	1970s		~45 ft	R-L	3,500 4,175 3,400	3 MIRV × 1–2 MT 1 RV 7 MIRV
(several) Typhoon	SS-NX-20	1980s		~45 ft		~4,330	12 MIRV
France							
5 *Le Redoubtable*	M-2 M-20	1976 1980s	44,000 lbs 44,000 lbs	34 ft 34 ft	R-S R-S	1,500 1,500	1 RV × 500 KT 1 RV × 1.2 MT + penetration aides
(1) *L'Inflexible*	M-4	1980s	~79,000 lbs	34 ft	R-S	2,100	6 MIRV × 100-KT

[a] See Appendix E for number of missiles carried by each submarine type.

[b] R = Rocket; S = Solid; L = Storable Liquid Propellant.

[c] Approximate range with full MIRV payload; range increases to about 2,500 n. miles with reduced number of RVs.

[d] Nine *Ohio* class submarines were under construction or authorized in 1982; all to initially carry the C-4 missiles with the D-5 to be retrofitted from 1989.

[e] US-NATO missile designations; the Soviet designation for the SS-N-18 is RSM-50.

APPENDIX D
Strategic Cruise Missiles (1982)

Designation	Launch Platforms	IOC	Launch Weight	Engines[a]	Range (n.mi)	Warhead/Notes
United States						
AGM-69B SRAM[b]	B-52G/H FB-111A	1972	2,200 lbs	R-S	100	200 KT
BGM-109 Tomahawk	submarines[c]	1980s	4,000 lbs	TF + booster	2,000+	nuclear or advanced conventional munitions as T-LAM (Land Attack Missile)
AGM-86B ALCM[d]	B-52	1980s	2,800 lbs	TF	1,500+	nuclear
Soviet Union						
AS-3 Kangaroo	Tu-20	early 1960s	~22,000 lbs	TJ	200+	nuclear
AS-4 Kitchen[e]	Tu-22 Tu-22M	early 1960s	~15,000 lbs	TJ	175	nuclear or conventional
AS-5 Kelt[e]	Tu-16	1965	~10,500 lbs	R-L	100+	nuclear or conventional
AS-6 Kingfish[e]	Tu-16	1970	~11,000 lbs	TJ	100+	nuclear or conventional
SS-N-3 Shaddock	submarines[f] surface ships	1961	~10,000 lbs	TJ	280[g] / 400+	nuclear or conventional
SS-N-12	submarines[f] surface ships	1979		TJ	200+	nuclear or conventional

[a] R = Rocket; TF = Turbofan; TJ = Turbojet; S = Solid propellant; L = Storable Liquid propellant.
[b] Short-Range Attack Missile.
[c] The Tomahawk can be launched from standard submarine torpedo tubes; does not require a specialized missile submarine.
[d] Air-Launched Cruise Missile.
[e] Apparently capable of being used against land or surface ship targets.
[f] See Appendix E for missile submarines.
[g] Anti-ship/land-attack ranges.

APPENDIX E
Strategic Missile Submarines (1982)

Number Operational	Name-Class	IOC	Submerged Displacement	Length Overall	Propulsion[a]	Missiles
United States						
31	*Lafayette*	1963	8,250 tons	425 ft	N	16 Poseidon C-3 or 16 Trident D-4
1[b]	*Ohio*	1982	18,700 tons	560 ft	N	24 Trident D-4 or D-5
Great Britain						
4	*Resolution*	1967	8,400 tons	425 ft	N	16 Polaris A-3
Soviet Union						
3	Golf-I	1958	2,850 tons	321 ft	DE	3 SS-N-4 Sark in Golf-I
13	Golf-II					3 SS-N-5 Serb in Golf-II
1	Golf-III					4 SS-N-8 in Golf-III
1	Golf-IV					5 SS-N-6 in Golf-IV
7	Hotel-II	1959	5,600 tons	377 ft	N	3 SS-N-5 Serb in Hotel-II
1	Hotel-III					6 SS-N-8 in Hotel-III
3	Yankee	1968	9,300 tons	428 ft	N	16 SS-N-6 in some Yankees 16 SS-N-16 in most Yankees 1 SS-NX-17 in 1 Yankee
19	Delta-I	1973	9,000 + tons	446 ft	N	12 SS-N-8
4	Delta-II	early 1970s	~12,000 tons	498 1/2 ft	N	16 SS-N-8
11[b]	Delta-III	mid 1970s	~12,000 tons	498 1/2 ft	N	16 SS-N-18
1[b]	Typhoon	1981	25,000 tons	600 + ft	N	20 SS-NX-20 (initially may carry SS-N-18)
16	Juliett	1961	3,550 tons	284 ft	DE	4 SS-N-3 cruise missiles
29	Echo-II	1960	5,800 tons	385 ft	N	8 SS-N-3 or SS-N-12 cruise missiles
France						
5	*Le Redoubtable*	1971	9,000 tons	420 ft	N	16 M-2 or M-20
(1)[b]	*L'Inflexible*	1985			N	16 M-4

[a] N = Nuclear; DE = Diesel-Electric.
[b] Additional units under construction.

National Strategy Information Center, Inc.

PUBLICATIONS

Gerald L. Steibel, Editor
Dorothy E. Nicolosi, Associate Editor
Joyce E. Larson, Managing Editor

STRATEGY PAPERS

Strategic Weapons: An Introduction by Norman Polmar, October 1975. Revised edition, June 1982

Conventional War and Escalation: The Soviet View by Joseph D. Douglass, Jr. and Amoretta M. Hoeber, November 1981

Soviet Perceptions of Military Doctrine and Military Power: The Interaction of Theory and Practice by John J. Dziak, June 1981

How Little is Enough? SALT and Security in the Long Run by Francis P. Hoeber, January 1981

Raw Material Supply in a Multipolar World by Yuan-li Wu, October 1973. Revised edition, October 1979

India: Emergent Power? by Stephen P. Cohen and Richard L. Park, June 1978

The Kremlin and Labor: A Study in National Security Policy by Roy Godson, November 1977

The Evolution of Soviet Security Strategy 1965-1975 by Avigdor Haselkorn, November 1977

The Geopolitics of the Nuclear Era by Colin S. Gray, September 1977

The Sino-Soviet Confrontation: Implications for the Future by Harold C. Hinton, September 1976 (Out of print)

Food, Foreign Policy, and Raw Materials Cartels by William Schneider, Jr., February 1976

Soviet Sources of Military Doctrine and Strategy by William F. Scott, July 1975

Detente: Promises and Pitfalls by Gerald L. Steibel, March 1975 (Out of print)

Oil, Politics and Sea Power: The Indian Ocean Vortex by Ian W.A.C. Adie, December 1974 (Out of print)

The Soviet Presence in Latin America by James D. Theberge, June 1974

The Horn of Africa by J. Bowyer Bell, Jr., December 1973

Research and Development and the Prospects for International Security by Frederick Seitz and Rodney W. Nichols, December 1973

The People's Liberation Army: Communist China's Armed Forces by Angus M. Fraser, August 1973 (Out of print)

Nuclear Weapons and the Atlantic Alliance by Wynfred Joshua, May 1973 (Out of print)

How to Think About Arms Control and Disarmament by James E. Dougherty, May 1973 (Out of print)

The Military Indoctrination of Soviet Youth by Leon Goure, January 1973 (Out of print)

The Asian Alliance: Japan and United States Policy by Franz Michael and Gaston J. Sigur, October 1972 (Out of print)

Iran, the Arabian Peninsula, and the Indian Ocean by R.M. Burrell and Alvin J. Cottrell, September 1972 (Out of print)

Soviet Naval Power: Challenge for the 1970s by Norman Polmar, April 1972. Revised edition, September 1974 (Out of print)

How Can We Negotiate with the Communists? by Gerald L. Steibel, March 1972 (Out of print)

Soviet Political Warfare Techniques, Espionage and Propaganda in the 1970s by Lyman B. Kirkpatrick, Jr., and Howland H. Sargeant, January 1972 (Out of print)

The Soviet Presence in the Eastern Mediterranean by Lawrence L. Whetten, September 1971 (Out of print)

The Military Unbalance: Is the U.S. Becoming a Second Class Power? June 1971 (Out of print)

The Future of South Vietnam by Brigadier F.P. Serong, February 1971 (Out of print)

Strategy and National Interests: Reflections for the Future by Bernard Brodie, January 1971 (Out of print)

The Mekong River: A Challenge in Peaceful Development for Southeast Asia by Eugene R. Black, December 1970 (Out of print)

Problems of Strategy in the Pacific and Indian Oceans by George C. Thomson, October 1970 (Out of print)

Soviet Penetration into the Middle East by Wynfred Joshua, July 1970. Revised edition, October 1971 (Out of print)

Australian Security Policies and Problems by Justus M. van der Kroef, May 1970 (Out of print)

Detente: Dilemma or Disaster? by Gerald L. Steibel, July 1969 (Out of print)

The Prudent Case for Safeguard by William R. Kintner, June 1969 (Out of print)

AGENDA PAPERS

The China Sea: The American Stake in its Future by Harold C. Hinton, January 1981

NATO, Turkey, and the Southern Flank: A Mideastern Perspective by Ihsan Gürkan, March 1980

The Soviet Threat to NATO's Northern Flank by Marian K. Leighton, November 1979

Does Defense Beggar Welfare? Myths Versus Realities by James L. Clayton, June 1979 (Out of print)

Naval Race or Arms Control in the Indian Ocean? (Some Problems in Negotiating Naval Limitations) by Alvin J. Cottrell and Walter F. Hahn, September 1978 (Out of print)

Power Projection: A Net Assessment of U.S. and Soviet Capabilities by W. Scott Thompson, April 1978

Understanding the Soviet Military Threat, How CIA Estimates Went Astray by William T. Lee, February 1977 (Out of print)

Toward a New Defense for NATO, The Case for Tactical Nuclear Weapons, July 1976 (Out of print)

Seven Tracks to Peace in the Middle East by Frank R. Barnett, April 1975

Arms Treaties with Moscow: Unequal Terms Unevenly Applied? by Donald G. Brennan, April 1975 (Out of print)

Toward a U.S. Energy Policy by Klaus Knorr, March 1975 (Out of print)

Can We Avert Economic Warfare in Raw Materials? US Agriculture as a Blue Chip by William Schneider, Jr., July 1974

BOOKS

Arms, Men, and Military Budgets: Issues for Fiscal Year 1981 by Francis P. Hoeber, William Schneider, Jr., Norman Polmar, and Ray Bessette, May 1980

Arms, Men, and Military Budgets: Issues for Fiscal Year 1979 by Francis P. Hoeber, David B. Kassing, and William Schneider, Jr., February 1978

Arms, Men, and Military Budgets: Issues for Fiscal Year 1978 edited by Francis P. Hoeber and William Schneider, Jr., May 1977

Arms, Men, and Military Budgets: Issues for Fiscal Year 1977 edited by William Schneider, Jr., and Francis P. Hoeber, May 1976 (Out of print)

*   *   *

Intelligence Requirements for the 1980s: Covert Action (Volume IV of a Series) edited by Roy Godson, September 1981

Intelligence Requirements for the 1980s: Counterintelligence (Volume III of a Series) edited by Roy Godson, January 1981

Intelligence Requirements for the 1980s: Analysis and Estimates (Volume II of a Series) edited by Roy Godson, June 1980

Intelligence Requirements for the 1980s: Elements of Intelligence (Volume I of a Series) edited by Roy Godson, October 1979

*   *   *

Our Changing Geopolitical Premises by Thomas P. Rona, January 1982

Strategic Minerals: A Resource Crisis published by the Council on Economics and National Security (an NSIC Project), December 1981

U.S. Policy and Low-Intensity Conflict: Potentials for Military Struggles in the 1980s edited by Sam C. Sarkesian and William L. Scully, June 1981

New Foundations for Asian and Pacific Security edited by Joyce E. Larson, September 1980

The Fateful Ends and Shades of SALT: Past . . . Present . . . And Yet to Come? by Paul H. Nitze, James E. Dougherty, and Francis X. Kane, March 1979

Strategic Options for the Early Eighties: What Can Be Done? edited by William R. Van Cleave and W. Scott Thompson, February 1979

Oil, Divestiture and National Security edited by Frank N. Trager, December 1976 (Out of print)

Indian Ocean Naval Limitations, Regional Issues and Global Implications by Alvin J. Cottrell and Walter F. Hahn, April 1976